THE PSALMS

28 September '81

Robert —

Be freed from

darkness and

heavy burdens,

enlightened

and lightened.

with love,

Jim

Rosh Hashanah

5742

THE PSALMS OF THE
JERUSALEM BIBLE

IMAGE BOOKS

A Division of Doubleday & Company, Inc.

Garden City, New York

Image Books edition 1970
by special arrangement with Doubleday & Company, Inc.
Image Books edition published September, 1970

The Psalms contained in this volume are from the Jerusalem Bible. The text of the Psalms and the notes have been reproduced complete and unabridged.

The introductions and notes of the Jerusalem Bible are, with minor variations and revisions, a translation of those which appeared in *La Bible de Jérusalem* published by Les Editions du Cerf, Paris (one volume edition, 1961, but modified in the light of the subsequent revised fascicule edition), under the general editorship of Père Roland de Vaux, O.P. The English text of the Bible itself, though translated from the ancient texts, owes a large debt to the work of the many scholars who collaborated to produce *La Bible de Jérusalem*, a debt which the publishers of this English Bible gratefully acknowledge.

INTRODUCTION TO
THE PSALMS

Lyric poetry in all its forms was popular in Israel from the earliest times, as it was among her neighbors in Egypt, Mesopotamia, and Canaan. Some samples are to be found in the historical books: the Song of Moses, Exodus 15, the Song of the Well, Numbers 21:17–18, the victory song of Deborah, Judges 5, David's elegy on Saul and Jonathan, 2 Samuel 1, etc., and many years later the panegyric of Judas Maccabaeus, 1 Maccabees 3:3–9, and of his brother Simon, 1 Maccabees 14:4–15; in the New Testament, the Magnificat, Benedictus, and Nunc Dimittis. In the prophetic books many passages belong to the same type of literature. Ancient collections once existed of which only the name or a few scraps survive: the Book of the Wars of Yahweh, Numbers 21:14, and the Book of the Just, Joshua 10:13; 2 Samuel 1:18. But the bulk of the religious poetry of Israel is preserved in the Psalter.

DESIGNATION

The Psalter (Greek, *Psalterion*, the string instrument used for the accompaniment of these songs or psalms) is a collection of one hundred and fifty psalms. From Psalm 10 to Psalm 148 the numbering of the Hebrew Bible (adopted here) is one figure ahead of the Greek and the Vulgate which join 9 and 10 and also 114 and 115, but divide both 116 and 147 into two.

The Hebrew name for the Psalter is *Tehillim*, "Hymns," but this designation fits only a certain number of psalms. In the "inscriptions" at the head of most of the psalms the word "hymn" is in fact used only once (Psalm 145). The usual inscription is *mizmor*, which implies musical accompaniment; our word "psalm" is therefore apt. Some of these "psalms" are also entitled "songs," and this term, standing alone, is found in the inscription of every psalm in the collection known as the "Songs of Ascents," 120–134. Other designations are less frequent and sometimes difficult to explain.

LITERARY FORMS

A more satisfying classification is obtained by study of the various literary types of which there are, broadly speaking, three: hymn, entreaty, thanksgiving. The classification is not exhaustive since there are secondary forms which are exceptional or composite; nor does it always correspond to a grouping of the psalms by subject matter or purpose.

1. *Hymns* (Psalms 8, 19, 29, 33, 46–48, 76, 84, 87, 93, 96–100, 103–106, 113, 114, 117, 122, 135, 136, 145–150). Their structure is fairly uniform. Each opens with an invitation to praise God. The body of the hymn indicates motives for praise, the wonders of God as shown in nature, particularly in his work of creation, and as shown in human history, particularly in his saving work for his people. The conclusion either repeats the introductory formula or expresses a prayer.

Within this group two subdivisions may be identified according to subject matter. The "Songs of Zion," 46, 48, 76, 87, in markedly eschatological terms, hymn the glories of the Holy City, which is both dwelling place of the Most High and goal of pilgrimage, cf. 84 and 122. The "Psalms of the Kingship of God," particularly 47, 93, 96–98, in a style reminiscent of the prophets, celebrate the universal sovereignty of Yahweh. Since they make use of the vocabulary and metaphors of human coronation ceremonies, the theory has been advanced that these were associated with a feast of the Enthroning of Yahweh possibly celebrated annually in Israel as the Enthroning of Marduk was in Babylon. But there is little evidence of the existence of such a feast in Israel.

2. *Entreaty.* These supplicatory psalms (or psalms of suffering, laments), unlike the hymns, do not celebrate the glories of God but are addressed directly to him. They usually begin by invoking God, adding either an appeal for help, a prayer, or an expression of confidence. In the body of the psalm an effort is made to win God's sympathy by a description of the psalmist's misfortunes. Here conventional figures of speech are used, so that it is rarely possible to define the historical or personal background of the prayer: waters of the abyss, snares of death or of Sheol, savage beasts (lions, bulls, dogs) symbolizing the psalmist's enemies, bones that grow dry or break, heart wildly beating and overcome with fear; all these conventional images recur. In these psalms there are protestations of innocence, 7, 12, 26, and acknowledgment of sin as in the Miserere, 51, and the other penitential psalms. God is reminded of his former kindnesses or reproached for his seeming absence or forgetfulness, 9–10, 22, 44. But expressions of persistent confidence are also common, 3, 5, 42–43, 55–57, 63, 130, etc., and at times the psalm of entreaty is one long confident appeal, 4, 11, 16, 23, 62, 121, 125, 131. Not infrequently the entreaty ends, abruptly on occasion, with a sense of assurance that the prayer is heard, and with an act of thanksgiving, 6, 22, 69, 140.

These entreaties may be collective or individual.

a. *Collective entreaties* (Psalms 12, 44, 60, 74, 79, 80, 83, 85, 106, 123, 129, 137). Some national catastrophe is the occasion: defeat, the destruction of Jerusalem, a national emergency; on these occasions God is entreated to save and restore his people. Two psalms at least, 74 and 137, as also the collection of lamentations attributed to Jeremiah, reflect the situation after the destruction of Jerusalem in 587, and 85 expresses the emotions of those who came back from exile. Psalm 106 is a general confession of the sins of the nation.

b. *Individual entreaties* (Psalms 3, 5–7, 13, 17, 22, 25, 26, 28, 31, 35, 38, 42–43, 51, 54–57, 59, 63, 64, 69–71, 77, 86, 102, 120, 130, 140–143). This type is especially common and the content widely varied: besides the perils of death, persecution, exile, and senility, these individual prayers beg for deliverance in particular from sickness, slander, and sin. The enemies complained of, or denounced, "those who do evil," are barely defined; but whoever they may be, they are certainly not sorcerers, as some have thought, whose spells these psalms are intended to repel. It was at one time thought that the "I" of these psalms was collective; this is not the case. Nor is it always the king speaking in the name of the people, as has been recently suggested. The accent is too individual and the absence of allusion to the king's person or office too marked to make these theories tenable. It is doubtless true that several of these psalms have been adapted to serve as national laments, thus 22, 28, 59, 69, 71, 102; it is also true that some, which we shall discuss later, are "royal" psalms; and lastly, it is true that all of these psalms did ultimately come into collective use (which is why they are found in the Psalter). Nonetheless, these prayers were composed for, or by, individuals to meet individual needs; the faith they express is entirely personal, and their entreaty comes straight from the heart.

3. *Thanksgiving.* The psalms of entreaty may end, as we have seen, with gratitude to God for granting the request. In the thanksgiving psalms this gratitude becomes the main theme. These are relatively few in number: 18, 21, 30, 33, 34, 40, 65–68, 92, 116, 118, 124, 129, 138, 144. Some are collective, others individual. The people as a whole thanks God for danger averted, a successful harvest, divine favor shown to the king. The individual, having recalled past distress and God's answer to his prayer, expresses his gratitude and exhorts all good men to join him in praising God. This

8

last is often the occasion for a doctrinal development. The literary structure of the thanksgiving psalms resembles that of the hymns.

4. *Exceptional and composite forms.* The three forms we have just described are not in watertight compartments: there is very often a mutual infiltration. Lamentation may be preceded by confident prayer, 27, 31, or followed by thanksgiving, 28, 57. Psalm 89 begins as a hymn, passes into a long prophetic oracle and ends with a lament. Psalm 119 throughout is a hymn to the Law but it is also an individual lament and it develops a theme of the wisdom literature. This last characteristic, already noticed in certain thanksgiving psalms, shows that not a few topics are found in the Psalter which in themselves are unnatural to lyric poetry. Wisdom themes may take such a prominent place that we speak, somewhat inaccurately, of "Didactic Psalms." Psalms 1, 112, 127, are wisdom literature pure and simple. Other psalms, however, preserve something of their lyrical quality: 25 is akin to the lamentations, 32, 37, 73, to the thanksgiving psalms, etc.

Certain other psalms have incorporated prophetic oracles, or are simply expanded oracles, 2, 50, 75, 81, 82, 85, 95, 110. These have recently been explained as actual oracles delivered in the course of Temple ceremonies by priest or prophet. But it is still often maintained that they had no direct connection with the Temple worship and merely adopted the prophetic style. It is an open question; but there is no doubt that on the one hand the relationship between Psalms and prophetic literature extends beyond the oracles themselves to many other themes (theophanies, metaphors of fire, chalice, crucible, etc.) and, on the other hand, that some connection must be recognized between Psalms and Temple worship. We shall return to this point.

We have already drawn attention to the prophetic element in the Psalter by mentioning the eschatological character of the Songs of Zion and of the Psalms of the Kingship of God. The universal renewal foretold by these poems is the messianic age; other psalms, more specifically, speak of the Messiah in person.

Scattered throughout the Psalter, and of varying literary form, is a group of royal psalms. These are divine oracles addressed to the king, 2, 110, prayers for the king, 20, 61, 72, 84, a thanksgiving for the king, 21, prayers of the king himself, 18, 28, 63, 101, a royal procession song, 132, a hymn of the king, 144, even a bridal ode for a royal marriage, 45. They are ancient poems dating from the time of the monarchy and reflecting the idiom and ceremonial of the court. As originally composed they referred to the king as a contemporary, and had a royal successor to David in mind, or even (45 according to one theory) a monarch of the Northern Kingdom.

But the king of the chosen people is divinely anointed (in Hebrew a "messiah," an anointed one); he is the recipient of God's blessing, and this blessing ensures the prosperity of his people. But this is not all. The divine promises to the dynasty of David made it possible to glimpse, beyond this king, another and privileged descendant of David, in whom God would take particular delight and whom he would designate to do his saving work. This king is the Anointed without equal, the Messiah. The prophecy of Nathan, 2 Samuel 7, is the first in this series of prophecies relating to the Messiah, son of David. This promise was essentially a promise of stability for the House of David, and this is the sense in which Psalms 89:29–38 and 132:11–12 quote it; but it was not long before it was interpreted as referring to an individual, and thus in Acts 2:30 comes to be applied to Christ.

It was natural, therefore, for some of these ancient royal songs, remaining in use after the fall of the monarchy, and included with minor adjustments and additions in the Psalter, to become messianic psalms in the strictest sense of the word. The messianic character of 2, 72, 110 is plain; and 110 is more frequently quoted in the New Testament than any other psalm. Even the wedding song of 45, interpreted in the light of the marriage allegory beloved of the prophets, came to express the union of the Messiah with his new Israel, and Hebrews 1:8 applies it to Christ. Following the same trend, the New Testament and early Christian tradition apply other psalms to Christ which, although not royal psalms, anticipated the situation and mind of the Messiah, the essentially Good Man, thus 16 and 22 and selected passages from many psalms, particularly 8, 35, 40, 41, 68, 69, 97, 102, 118, 119. Similarly, the Kingship Psalms have been applied to the kingship of Christ. Even if these applications go beyond the immediate literal sense of the text applied, they are legitimate in that the hopes inspiring the Psalter could not be fully realized until the coming of the Son of God to earth.

THE PSALMS AND PUBLIC WORSHIP

The Psalter is Israel's hymnbook. The Temple, as we know, had its cantors from the beginning, though they are not mentioned until after the Exile. The festivals of Yahweh were celebrated with song and dance, Judges 21:19–21; 2 Samuel 6:5, 16. According to Amos 5:23, sacrifice was offered to the accompaniment of song, and since the court had its cantors in David's day, 2 Samuel 19:36, and (according to the Annals of Sennacherib) in the time of Hezekiah, the Temple of Solomon like all the great sanctuaries of the East must have had its cantors also. Psalms are in fact attributed to Asaph, to the sons of Korah, to Heman and to Ethan (or Jeduthun) who, according to Chronicles, were all cantors in the pre-exilic Temple. Tradition attributes many psalms to David and also credits him with organizing public worship, including the cantors, 1 Chronicles 25; and this harmonizes with those ancient texts representing him as dancing and singing in the presence of Yahweh, 2 Samuel 6:5, 16.

Many of the psalms carry musical or liturgical directions. The text of some refers to a public liturgy, 20, 26, 27, 66, 81, 107, 116, 134, 135. These last, and others, 48, 65, 95, 96, 118, were evidently recited in the Temple court. The Songs of Ascents, 120–134, like 84, were songs used on the Temple pilgrimage. These are some of the clearest examples, but are enough to show that many psalms, even individual psalms, were composed for Temple worship. Others, if not composed primarily for this purpose, have at least been adapted for it by the addition of benedictions, 125, 128, 129.

It is therefore certain that the psalms were related to public worship and that the Psalter, taken as a whole, is liturgical in character. But there is rarely enough evidence to identify the ceremony or feast for which any given psalm was used. The Hebrew title of 92 assigns it to the sabbath day, and the Greek titles of 24, 48, 93, 94 apportion them severally to other days of the week. Psalm 30 was used, according to the Hebrew, for the feast of Dedication, and 29, according to the Greek, for the feast of Tabernacles. These instructions are perhaps later additions, but, like the detailed allocations made in the Jewish period, prove that the Psalter was the hymnbook of Temple and synagogue before it was adopted by the Christian Church.

AUTHORS AND DATES

The inscriptions attribute seventy-three psalms to David, twelve to Asaph, eleven to the sons of Korah, one each to

Heman, Ethan (or Jeduthun), Moses, and Solomon. The inscriptions in the Greek version do not always correspond with the Hebrew text and credit David with eighty-two psalms. The Syriac version shows still greater divergence.

It is possible that the original purpose of these inscriptions was not to name the actual author. The Hebrew formula used merely establishes some kind of relationship between the psalm and the person named, either because of an aptness of theme or because the psalm belonged to a collection named after him. The psalms "for (or 'of') the sons of Korah" were part of the repertoire of this family of cantors, just as the numerous psalms "for the choirmaster," 4, 5, 6, 8, etc., were pieces performed under his direction. Similarly there was Asaph's collection and a Davidic collection. But it was not long before these notices of origin were taken to be indications of authorship, and to the inscription "of David" at the head of some psalms were added details of the exact circumstances in the life of the king at the time when these psalms were composed, 3, 7, 18, 34, 51, 52, 54, etc. Finally tradition made David the author not only of the psalms that bear his name but of the whole Psalter.

Notwithstanding mistaken deductions of this kind, it would be wrong to neglect the ancient and valuable information embodied in the inscriptions. It is reasonable to admit that the collections of Asaph and the sons of Korah were composed by poets attached to the Temple. It is equally reasonable to hold that there must be some connection between the Davidic collection and David himself. Taking into account what the historical books have to say of his musical talent, 1 Samuel 16:16–18; cf. Amos 6:5, his poetic gifts, 2 Samuel 1:19–27; 3:33–34, and his love of the liturgy, 2 Samuel 6:5, 15–16, it would seem inevitable that the Psalter should contain some of David's compositions. Indeed, Psalm 18 is simply a different edition of a poem attributed to David in 2 Samuel 22. Not all the psalms of the Davidic collection are by him, no doubt, but the collection must have had a few of these for nucleus. It is difficult, however, to be more definite than this. The Hebrew inscriptions are not decisive, as we have seen, and when the New Testament writers quote a psalm as being by David, they are speaking as their contemporaries spoke. Even so, this evidence should not be rejected without good reason, and David, who "sang the songs of Israel," 2 Samuel 23:1, must be conceded an essential part in the formation of the religious poetry of the Chosen People.

The original impulse given by David continued to have effects and the Psalter covers several centuries of poetic activity. After an erroneous assessment, assigning a very late date to the majority of the psalms, more moderate views now prevail. Apart from those psalms which may have been composed by David, many go back to the monarchical period, in particular all the royal psalms, but their content is too general for more than conjectural dating. The Psalms of the Kingship of God, on the other hand, with their many echoes of earlier psalms and of the second part of Isaiah, must have been written during the Exile, as also those, such as 137, which speak of the destruction of Jerusalem and the deportation. Psalm 126 celebrates the return from exile. The period that followed seems to have been fertile in psalmody. The restored Temple saw a reflorescence of public worship, the status of the cantors was so raised that they became assimilated with the Levites, while sages like Ben Sira adopted psalm form to popularize their teaching. Are any psalms of later date than the end of the Persian period? Are there any Maccabaean psalms? The question arises in particular connection with 44, 74, 79, 83, but the arguments advanced are not strong enough to prove so late a date of composition.

FORMATION OF THE PSALTER

The Psalter as we have it is the result of lengthy activity. At first there were partial collections. Psalm 72 (though its title assigns it to Solomon) is followed by the note: "End of the prayers of David," although there are non-Davidic psalms before it and Davidic psalms after it. In fact there are two Davidic groups, 3–41 and 51–72, in which every psalm (except 72 and four anonymous psalms) is attributed to David. Originally there must have been other separate collections of the same sort: the psalters of Asaph, 50 and 73–83, of the sons of Korah, 42–49 and 84, 85, 87, 88, of Ascents, 120–134, of the Hallel, 105–107, 113–118, 135, 136, 146–150. That there were several collections existing side by side is proved by the way certain psalms duplicate each other almost word for word, thus 14 and 53; 40:13–17 and 70; 108 with 57:7–11 and 60:5–12.

Furthermore, the activities of the collectors can be detected in the use of the divine names: "Yahweh" is almost exclusively used in 1–41 (first Davidic group), "Elohim" in 42–83 (covering the second Davidic group; part of the psalter of the sons of Korah; psalter of Asaph), all the remainder are "Yahwistic" with the exception of 108 (combination of the two "Elohistic" psalms 57 and 60). This second "Yahwistic" group, in which many of the psalms are anonymous and in which there is considerable quotation of, or borrowing from, earlier literature, must be the most recent group of all; though this does not prejudice the dating of individual psalms within the group.

The Psalter was ultimately divided into five books, doubtless on the model of the Pentateuch; the books were divided from each other by short doxologies: 41:13; 72:18–20; 89:51; 106:48. Psalm 150 is a protracted final doxology while 1 serves as an introduction to the whole Psalter.

SPIRITUAL VALUE

The spiritual riches of the Psalter need no commendation. The psalms were the prayers of the Old Testament in which God inspired the feeling that his children ought to have toward him and the words they ought to use when speaking to him. They were recited by Jesus himself, by the Virgin Mary, the apostles, and the early martyrs. The Christian Church has adopted them unchanged for her official prayer. Unchanged: the cries of praise, entreaty, and thanksgiving, wrung from the psalmists by events of their own times and by their personal experiences, have a universal note, expressing as they do the attitude that every man should have toward God. Unchanged as regards the words, but with a great enrichment of the sense: in the New Covenant, the faithful man praises and thanks God for unveiling the secret of his inmost nature, for redeeming him by the blood of his Son, for filling him with his Spirit; hence each psalm ends with the trinitarian doxology: *Glory be to the Father and to the Son and to the Holy Spirit*. The ancient entreaties have become more ardent since the last supper, the cross, and the resurrection have taught mankind the infinite quality of the love of God, the universality and gravity of sin, the glory promised to the faithful. The hopes sung by the psalmists have been fulfilled, the Messiah has come, he reigns and all nations are summoned to praise him.

THE PSALMS

PSALM 1[a]

The two ways

1 Happy the man
who never follows the advice of the wicked,
or loiters on the way that sinners take,
or sits about with scoffers,
2 but finds his pleasure in the Law of Yahweh,
and murmurs[b] his law day and night.

3 He is like a tree that is planted
by water streams,
yielding its fruit in season,
its leaves never fading;
success attends all he does.
4 It is nothing like this with the wicked, nothing like this!

No, these are like chaff
blown away by the wind.
5 The wicked will not stand firm when Judgment comes,[c]
nor sinners when the virtuous assemble.
6 For Yahweh takes care of the way the virtuous go,
but the way of the wicked is doomed.

PSALM 2

The messianic drama[a]

1 Why this uproar among the nations?
  Why this impotent muttering of pagans—
2 kings on earth rising in revolt,
  princes plotting against Yahweh and his Anointed,
3 "Now let us break their fetters!
  Now let us throw off their yoke!"

4 The One whose throne is in heaven sits laughing,
  Yahweh derides them.
5 Then angrily he addresses them,
  in a rage he strikes them with panic,
6 "This is my king, installed by me
  on Zion, my holy mountain."

7   Let me[b] proclaim Yahweh's decree;
  he has told me, "You are my son,
  today I have become your father.
8 Ask and I will give you the nations for your heritage,
  the ends of the earth for your domain.
9 With iron scepter you will break them,
  shatter them like potter's ware."[c]

10 So now, you kings, learn wisdom,
  earthly rulers, be warned:
11 serve Yahweh, fear him,
12 tremble and kiss his feet,[d]
  or he will be angry and you will perish,
  for his anger is very quick to blaze.

Happy all who take shelter in him.

PSALM 3

Morning prayer of the virtuous man under persecution

*Psalm – Of David – When he was escaping from
his son Absalom*

1 Yahweh, more and more are turning against me,
  more and more rebelling against me,
2 more and more saying about me,
  "There is no help for him in his God."   *Pause*

3 But, Yahweh, my encircling shield,
  my glory, you help me hold up my head.
4 Loudly I cry to Yahweh,
  and he answers me from his holy mountain.   *Pause*

5 Now I can lie down and go to sleep
  and then awake, for Yahweh has hold of me:[a]
6 no fear now of those tens of thousands
  posted against me wherever I turn.

7 Rise, Yahweh!
  Save me, my God!
  You hack all my enemies to the cheekbone,
  you break the teeth of the wicked.
8 From Yahweh, rescue.
  On your people, blessing!   *Pause*

PSALM 4

Evening prayer[a]

For the choirmaster — For strings — Psalm — Of David

1 God, guardian of my rights, you answer[b] when I call,
   when I am in trouble, you come to my relief;
   now be good to me and hear my prayer.

2 You men, why shut your hearts[c] so long,
   loving delusions, chasing after lies.   *Pause*
3 Know this, Yahweh works wonders for those he loves,
   Yahweh hears me when I call to him.

4   Tremble: give up sinning,
   spend your night in quiet meditation.[d]   *Pause*
5 Offer sacrifice in a right spirit, and trust Yahweh.

6 "Who will give us sight of happiness?" many say.
   Show us the light of your face, turned toward us![e]

7 Yahweh, you have given more joy to my heart
   than others ever knew, for all their corn and wine.

8 In peace I lie down, and fall asleep at once,
   since you alone, Yahweh, make me rest secure.

PSALM 5
Morning Prayer

For the choirmaster – For flutes – Psalm – Of David

1 Yahweh, let my words come to your ears,
    spare a thought for my sighs.
2 Listen to my cry for help,
    my King and my God!

3 I say this prayer to you, Yahweh,
    for at daybreak you listen for my voice;[a]
and at dawn I hold myself in readiness[b] for you,
    I watch for you.

4 You are not a God who is pleased with wickedness,
    you have no room for the wicked;
5 boasters collapse
    under your scrutiny.

You hate all evil men,
6   liars you destroy;
murderers and frauds
    Yahweh detests.

7 But I, so great is your love,
    may come to your house,
and before your holy Temple bow down
    in reverence to you.

8 Yahweh, lead me in the path of your righteousness,
    for there are men lying in wait for me;[c]
make your way plain before me.
9 Not a word from their lips can be trusted,
    deep within them lies ruin,

their throats are yawning graves;
    they make their tongues so smooth!

10 Pronounce them guilty,[a] God,
    make their intrigues their own downfall!
  Hound them for their countless crimes,
    since they have rebelled against you.

11 But joy for all who take shelter in you,
    endless shouts of joy!
  Since you protect them, they exult in you,
    those who love your name.

12 It is you who bless the virtuous man, Yahweh;
    your favor is like a shield covering him.

PSALM 6

Prayer in ordeal[a]

*For the choirmaster – For strings, for the octachord –
Psalm – Of David*

1 Yahweh, do not punish me in your rage,
  or reprove me in the heat of anger.
2 Pity me, Yahweh, I have no strength left,
  heal me, my bones are in torment,
3 my soul is in utter torment.
  Yahweh, how long will you be?

4 Come back, Yahweh, rescue my soul,[b]
  save me, if you love me;
5 for in death there is no remembrance of you:
  who can sing your praises in Sheol?[c]

6 I am worn out with groaning,
  every night I drench my pillow

and soak my bed with tears;
7 my eye is wasted with grief,
I have grown old with enemies all round me.[d]

8 Away from me, all you evil men!
For Yahweh has heard the sound of my weeping;
9 Yahweh has heard my petition,
Yahweh will accept my prayer.
10 Let all my enemies, discredited, in utter torment,
fall back in sudden confusion.

PSALM 7

Prayer of the virtuous under persecution[a]

*Lamentation—Of David, who sang it to Yahweh about
Cush[b] the Benjaminite*

1 Yahweh my God, I take shelter in you;
from all who hound me, save me, rescue me,
2 or, like a lion, he will carry me off
and tear me to pieces where no one can save me.

3 Yahweh my God, if I ever
soiled my hands with fraud,
4 repaid a friend evil for good,
spared a man who wronged me,[c]
5 then let the enemy hound me down and catch me,[d]
let him stamp my life into the ground,
and leave my entrails[e] lying in the dust!   *Pause*

6 Rise, Yahweh, in anger,
awake, my God![f]
Confront the raging of my enemies,
you who demand that justice shall be done.

7 Let the nations muster round you in a body,
      and then return, high over them.
8 (Yahweh is arbiter of nations.)*g*

   Give judgment for me, Yahweh: as my virtue
      and my integrity*h* deserve.
9 Bring the maliciousness of evil men to an end,
      set the virtuous on his feet,
      you righteous God,
   assessor of mind and heart.

10 God is the shield that protects me,
      he preserves upright hearts,
11 God the righteous judge
      is slow to show his anger,*i*
   but he is a God who is always enraged
12   by those who refuse to repent.

   The enemy*j* may sharpen his sword,
      he may bend his bow and take aim,
13 but the weapons he prepares will kill himself
      and his arrows turn into firebrands.
14 Look at him, pregnant with wickedness,
      conceiving Spite, he gives birth to Mishap.
15 He dug a pit, hollowed it out,
      only to fall into his own trap!
16 His spite recoils on his own head,
      his brutality falls back on his own skull.

17 I give thanks to Yahweh for his righteousness,
      I sing praise*k* to the name of the Most High.

PSALM 8

The munificence of the creator

*For the choirmaster – On the . . . of Gath[a] – Psalm – Of
David*

1 Yahweh, our Lord,
how great your name throughout the earth!

Above the heavens is your majesty chanted[b]
2 by the mouths of children, babes in arms.[c]
You set your stronghold[d] firm against your foes
to subdue enemies and rebels.

3 I look up at your heavens, made by your fingers,
at the moon and stars you set in place—
4 ah, what is man that you should spare a thought for him,
the son of man that you should care for him?
5 Yet you have made him little less than a god,[e]
you have crowned him with glory and splendor,
6 made him lord over the work of your hands,
set all things under his feet,

7 sheep and oxen, all these,
yes, wild animals too,
8 birds in the air, fish in the sea
traveling the paths of the ocean.[f]

9 Yahweh, our Lord,
how great your name throughout the earth!

PSALM 9–10

God crushes the wicked and saves the humble[a]

For the choirmaster – For oboe and harp[b] – Psalm – Of David

1 *Aleph* I thank you, Yahweh, with all my heart;
I recite your marvels one by one,
2 I rejoice and exult in you,
I sing praise to your name, Most High.

3 *Beth* My enemies are in retreat,
stumbling, perishing as you confront them:
4 you have upheld the justice of my cause
from the throne where you sit as righteous judge.[c]

5 *Ghimel* You have checked the nations, you have
crushed the wicked,
blotted out their name for ever and ever;
6 the enemy is finished, in everlasting ruin,
you have overthrown cities, their memory has perished.

7 *He* See,[d] Yahweh is enthroned for ever
he sets up his throne for judgment;
8 he is going to judge the world with justice,
and pronounce a true verdict on the nations.

9 *Waw* May Yahweh be a stronghold for the oppressed,
a stronghold when times are hard.
10 Those who acknowledge your name can rely on you,
you never desert those who seek you, Yahweh.

11 *Zain* To Yahweh with his home in Zion, sing praise,
tell the nations of his mighty actions;
12 he, the avenger of blood, remembers them,
he does not ignore the cry of the wretched.

¹³ *Heth* Take pity on me, Yahweh, look on my suffering,^e
you who lift me back from the gates of death,
¹⁴ that in the gates of the daughter of Zion
I may recite your praises one by one, rejoicing that you
have saved me.

¹⁵ *Teth* The nations have sunk into a pit of their own
making,
they are caught by the feet in the snare they set themselves.
¹⁶ Yahweh has made himself known, has given judgment,
he has trapped the wicked in the work of their own
hands.   *Muted music*

¹⁷ May the wicked return to Sheol,   *Pause*
all the nations forgetful of God.
¹⁸ *Kaph* For the needy is not always forgotten,
the hope of the poor is never brought to nothing.

¹⁹ Rise, Yahweh, let not man have the upper hand,
let the nations stand trial before you!
²⁰ Strike terror into them, Yahweh,
let the nations know they are only men!   *Pause*

10

¹ *Lamed* Yahweh, why do you stand aside,
why hide from us now the times are hard?
² The poor man is devoured by the pride of the wicked,^a
he is caught in the wiles that the other has devised.

³ (*Mem*) The evil man boasts of his soul's desires,
the grasping man blasphemes, the wicked spurns
Yahweh.
⁴ (*Nun*) "His anger is up there,^b he will not make me
pay!
There is no God!" This is the way his mind works.^c

⁵ At every moment his course is assured,
your rulings are too lofty for his notice;
his rivals? He sneers at them all.

6 "Nothing can shake me," he assures himself.
7 Himself untouched by disaster, he curses others.

(*Samek*) Fraud and oppression fill his mouth,
Pe spite and iniquity are under his tongue;
8 there in the reeds[d] he lies in ambush
to kill the innocent where no one can see.

Ain Peering and prying for the out-of-luck,
9 lurking unseen like a lion in his hide,
lurking to capture the poor man,
the poor man seized, he drags him away in his net.

10 (*Sade*) Questing of eye, he stoops, he crouches,
and the luckless wretch falls into his power[e]
11 as he thinks to himself, "God forgets,
he hides his face, he does not see at all."

12 *Qoph* Rise, Yahweh, God raise your hand,[f]
do not forget the poor!
13 why does the wicked man spurn God,
assuring himself, "He will not make me pay"?

14 *Resh* [g]You yourself have seen the distress and the grief,
you watch and then take them into your hands;
the luckless man commits himself to you,
you, the orphan's certain help.

15 *Shin* Break the power of the wicked, of the evil man,
seek out his wickedness till there is none to be found!
16 Yahweh is king for ever and ever,
the pagans are doomed to vanish from his country.

17 *Tau* Yahweh, you listen to the wants of the humble,
you bring strength to their hearts, you grant them a hearing,
18 judging in favor of the orphaned and exploited,
so that earthborn man may strike fear no longer.

PSALM 11

The confidence of the virtuous

For the choirmaster – Of David

1 In Yahweh I take shelter.
   How can you say to me,
   "Bird, fly back to your mountain:[a]

2 "see how the wicked are bending their bows
   and fitting their arrows to the string,
   ready to shoot the upright from the shadows.

3 When foundations fall to ruin, what can the virtuous do?"

4 Yahweh is in his holy Temple,
   Yahweh whose throne is in heaven;
   his eyes look down at the world,[b]
   his searching gaze scans all mankind.

5 The virtuous and the wicked are under Yahweh's scrutiny,
   and his soul hates anyone who loves brutality.

6 He rains coals of fire[c] and brimstone on the wicked,
   he serves them a scorching wind to swallow down.[d]

7 Yahweh is righteous, he loves virtue,
   upright men will contemplate his face.[e]

PSALM 12

Against a deceitful world[a]

For the choirmaster – For the octachord – Psalm – Of David

1 Save us, Yahweh! There are no devout men left,
  fidelity has vanished from mankind.
2 All they do is lie to one another,
  flattering lips, talk from a double heart.

3 May Yahweh slice off every flattering lip,
  each tongue so glib with boasts,
4 those who say, "In our tongue lies our strength,
  our lips have the advantage; who can master us?"

5 "For the plundered poor, for the needy who groan,
  now will I act," says Yahweh.
  "I will grant them the safety they sigh for."

6 The words of Yahweh are without alloy,
  nature's silver[b] coming from the earth seven times refined.
7 And you, Yahweh, hold us in your keeping,
  against that breed protect us always.
8 The wicked prowl on every side,
  baseness stands high[c] among the sons of men.

PSALM 13

A confident appeal

For the choirmaster – Psalm – Of David

1 How much longer will you forget me? Yahweh? For ever?
   How much longer will you hide your face from me?
2 How much longer must I endure grief in my soul,
   and sorrow in my heart by day and by night?
   How much longer must my enemy have the upper hand
   of me?
3 Look and answer me, Yahweh my God!

   Give my eyes light, or I shall sleep in death,
4 and my enemy will say, "I have beaten him,"
   and my oppressors have the joy of seeing me stumble.
5 But I for my part rely on your love, Yahweh;
   let my heart rejoice in your saving help.
   Let me sing to Yahweh for the goodness he has shown
   me.*a*

PSALM 14

The godless men*a*

For the choirmaster – Of David

1 The fool says in his heart,
   "There is no God!"
   Their deeds are corrupt and vile,
   there is not one good man left.

2 Yahweh is looking down from heaven
    at the sons of men,
to see if a single one is wise,
    if a single one is seeking God.

3 All have turned aside,
    all alike are tainted;
there is not one good man left,
    not a single one.[b]

4 Are they so ignorant, all these evil men
    who swallow my people[c]
as though they were eating bread,
    and never invoke Yahweh?

5 They will be struck with fear,
    fear without reason,[d]
since God takes the side of the virtuous:
6 deride as you may the poor man's hopes,
    Yahweh is his shelter.

7 Who will bring Israel salvation from Zion?
When Yahweh brings his people home,[e]
what joy for Jacob, what happiness for Israel!

PSALM 15   V 14

The guest of Yahweh[a]

Psalm – Of David

1 Yahweh, who has the right to enter your tent,
    or to live on your holy mountain?

2 The man whose way of life is blameless,
    who always does what is right,
    who speaks the truth from his heart,

3   whose tongue is not used for slander,
    who does no wrong to his fellow,
    casts no discredit on his neighbor,
4   looks with contempt on the reprobate,
    but honors those who fear Yahweh;[b]

    who stands by his pledge at any cost,
5   does not ask interest on loans,
    and cannot be bribed to victimize the innocent.
    —If a man does all this, nothing can ever shake him.

PSALM 16

Yahweh, my heritage

Miktam[a] – Of David

1   Look after me, God, I take shelter in you.

2   To Yahweh you[b] say, "My Lord,
    you are my fortune, nothing else but you,"
3   yet to those pagan deities in the land,
    "My princes, all my pleasure is in you."

4   Their idols teem, after these they run:[c]
    shall I pour their blood libations?—not I!
    Take their names on my lips?—never!

5   Yahweh, my heritage, my cup,
    you, and you only, hold my lot secure;
6   the measuring line marks out delightful places for me,
    for me the heritage is superb indeed.[d]
7   I bless Yahweh, who is my counselor,
    and in the night my inmost self[e] instructs me;
8   I keep Yahweh before me always,
    for with him at my right hand nothing can shake me.

33

9 So my heart exults, my very soul[f] rejoices,
    my body, too, will rest securely,
10 for you will not abandon my soul to Sheol,
    nor allow the one you love to see the Pit;[g]
11 you will reveal the path of life to me,
    give me unbounded joy in your presence,
    and at your right hand everlasting pleasures.

PSALM 17 V 16

The innocent man pleads his cause

Prayer – Of David

1   Yahweh, hear the plea of virtue,
        listen to my appeal,
    lend an ear to my prayer,
        my lips free from dishonesty.
2   From your presence will my sentence come,
        your eyes are fixed on what is right.

3 You probe my heart, examine me at night,
  you test me yet find nothing, no murmuring from me:
4 my mouth has never sinned as most men's do.

  No, I have treasured the words from your lips;
5 in the path prescribed walking deliberately
  in your footsteps, so that my feet do not slip.

6 I invoke you, God, and you answer me;
  turn your ear to me, hear what I say,
7 display your marvelous kindness, savior of fugitives!

  From those who revolt against you
8 guard me like the pupil of your eye;
  hide me in the shadow of your wings
9 from the onslaughts of the wicked.

My enemies cluster round me, breathing hostility;
10 entrenched in their fat, their mouths utter
11 arrogant claims; *now they are closing in,
they have eyes for nothing but to see me overthrown.
12 They look like a lion eager to tear to pieces,
like a young lion crouching in its hide.

13 Rise, Yahweh, subdue him face to face,
rescue my soul from the wicked with your sword,
14 with your hand, Yahweh, rescue me from men,
from the sort of men whose lot is here and now.*

Cram their bellies from your stores,*
give them all the sons that they could wish for,
let them have a surplus to leave their children!
15 For me the reward of virtue is to see your face,
and, on waking, to gaze my fill on your likeness.*

PSALM 18   V 17

Song of triumph for the king*

For the choirmaster. Of David, the servant of Yahweh, who addressed the words of this song to Yahweh at the time when Yahweh delivered him from the power of his enemies and of Saul. He said:

1 I love you, Yahweh, my strength
(my savior, you rescue me from violence.)*
2 Yahweh is my rock and my bastion,
my deliverer is my God.

I take shelter in him, my rock,*
my shield, my horn of salvation,*
my stronghold and my refuge.
From violence you rescue me.

35

³ He is to be praised; on Yahweh I call
  and am saved from my enemies.

⁴ The waves*ᵉ* of death encircled me,
  the torrents of Belial burst on me;
⁵ the cords of Sheol girdled me,
  the snares of death were before me.

⁶ In my distress I called to Yahweh
  and to my God I cried;
  from his Temple he heard my voice,
  my cry came to his ears.

⁷ Then the earth*ᶠ* quivered and quaked,
  the foundations of the mountains trembled
  (they quivered because he was angry);
⁸ from his nostrils a smoke ascended,
  and from his mouth a fire that consumed
  (live embers were kindled at it).

⁹ He bent the heavens and came down,
  a dark cloud under his feet;
¹⁰ he mounted a cherub*ᵍ* and flew,
  and soared on the wings of the wind.

¹¹ Darkness he made a veil to surround him,
  his tent a watery darkness, dense cloud;
¹² before him a flash enkindled
  hail and fiery embers.

¹³ Yahweh thundered from heaven,
  the Most High made his voice heard;
¹⁴ he let his arrows fly and scattered them,
  launched the lightnings and routed them.

¹⁵ The bed of the seas was revealed,
  the foundations of the world were laid bare,
  at your muttered threat, Yahweh,
  at the blast of your nostrils' breath.
¹⁶ He sends from on high and takes me,
  he draws me from deep waters,

17 he delivers me from my powerful enemy,
   from a foe too strong for me.

18 They assailed me on my day of disaster,
   but Yahweh was my support;
19 he freed me, set me at large,
   he rescued me, since he loves me.

20 Yahweh requites me as I act justly,
   as my hands are pure so he repays me,
21 since I have kept the ways of Yahweh,
   nor fallen away from my God.

22 His judgments are all before me,
   his statutes I have not put from me;
23 I am blameless in his presence,
   I keep sin at arm's length.

24 And Yahweh repays me as I act justly,
   as my purity is in his sight.
25 Faithful you are with the faithful,
   blameless with the blameless,
26 pure with the one who is pure,
   but crafty with the devious,
27 you save a people that is humble
   and humiliate eyes that are haughty.

28 Yahweh, you yourself are my lamp,[h]
   my God lights up my darkness;
29 with you I storm the barbican,
   with my God I leap the rampart.

30 This God, his way is blameless;
   the word of Yahweh is without dross.
   He it is who is the shield
   of all who take shelter in him.

31 Who else is God but Yahweh,
   who else a rock save our God?
32 This God who girds me with strength
   and makes my way without blame,

33 who makes my feet like the hinds'
   and holds me from falling on the heights,
34 who trains my hands for battle,
   my arms to bend a bow of bronze.

35 You give me your saving shield
   (your right hand upholds me), with care you train me,[i]
36 wide room you make for my steps under me,
   my feet have never faltered.

37 I pursue my enemies and overtake them,
   nor turn back till an end is made of them;
38 I strike them down, and they cannot rise,
   they fall, they are under my feet.

39 You have girt me with strength for the fight,
   bent down my assailants beneath me,
40 made my enemies turn their backs to me;
   and those who hate me I destroy.

41 They cry out, there is no one to save,
   to Yahweh, but there is no reply;
42 I crush them fine as dust before the wind,
   trample them like the mud of the streets.

43 You deliver me from a people in revolt,
   you place me at the head of the nations,
   a people I did not know are now my servants,

44 foreigners come wooing my favor,
   no sooner do they hear than they obey me,
45 foreigners grow faint of heart,
   they come trembling out of their fastnesses.

46 Life to Yahweh! Blessed be my rock!
   Exalted be the God of my salvation,
47 the God who gives me vengeance
   and subjects the peoples to me,
48 who rescues me from my raging enemies.
   You lift me high above those who attack me,
   you deliver me from the man of violence.

⁴⁹ For this I will praise you, Yahweh, among the heathen
and sing praise to your name.

⁵⁰ His king he saves and saves again,
displays his love for his anointed,
for David and his heirs for ever.

PSALM 19

V 18

Yahweh, the sun of righteousness^a

For the choirmaster – Psalm – Of David

¹ The heavens declare the glory of God,
the vault of heaven proclaims his handiwork;
² day discourses of it to day,
night to night hands on the knowledge.

³ No utterance at all, no speech,
no sound that anyone can hear;^b
⁴ yet their voice goes out through all the earth,
and their message to the ends of the world.

High above, he pitched a tent for the sun,
⁵ who comes out of his pavilion like a bridegroom,
exulting like a hero to run his race.^c

⁶ He has his rising on the edge of heaven,
the end of his course is its farthest edge,
and nothing can escape his heat.

⁷ The Law of Yahweh is perfect,
new life for the soul;
the decree of Yahweh is trustworthy,
wisdom for the simple.

8   The precepts of Yahweh are upright,
       joy for the heart;
    the commandment of Yahweh is clear,
       light for the eyes.

9   The fear of Yahweh is pure,
       lasting for ever;
    the judgments of Yahweh are true,
       righteous, every one,

10   more desirable than gold,
       even than the finest gold;
    his words[d] are sweeter than honey,
       even than honey that drips from the comb.

11   Thus your servant is formed by them,
       observance brings great reward.
12   But who can detect his own failings?
       Wash out my hidden faults.

13   And from pride[e] preserve your servant,
       never let it dominate me.
    So shall I be above reproach,
       free from grave sin.
14   May the words of my mouth always[f] find favor,
       and the whispering of my heart,
    in your presence, Yahweh,
       my Rock, my Redeemer![g]

PSALM 20   V 19

Prayer for the king[a]

For the choirmaster – Psalm – Of David

1   May Yahweh answer you in time of trouble,
    may the name of the God of Jacob protect you!

² May he send you help from the sanctuary,
  give you support from Zion,
³ remember all your oblations
  and find your holocaust acceptable;   *Pause*
⁴ may he grant you your heart's desire,
  and crown all your plans with success;
⁵ may we shout with joy for your victory,
  and plant our banners in the name of our God!

May Yahweh grant all your petitions!

⁶ Now I know that Yahweh
  saves his anointed,[b]
  and answers him from his holy heaven
  with mighty victories from his own right hand.

⁷ Some boast of chariots, some of horses,
  but we boast about the name of Yahweh our God;
⁸ theirs to crumple and fall,
  but we shall stand, and stand firm!

⁹ Yahweh, save the king,
  answer us[c] when we call.

PSALM 21   V 20

Thanksgiving for the king[a]

For the choirmaster – Psalm – Of David

¹ Yahweh, the king rejoices in your power;
  what great joy your saving help gives him!
² You have granted him his heart's desire,
  not denied him what his lips entreated.   *Pause*

³ For you have met him with choicest blessings,
  put a crown of pure gold on his head;

41

⁴ he asked for life, and you gave it him,
length of days for ever and ever.

⁵ Great his glory through your saving help,
you have loaded him with splendor and majesty;
⁶ yes, you confer on him everlasting blessings,
you gladden him with the joy of your presence.

⁷ Yes, the king puts his trust in Yahweh,
by grace of the Most High he reigns unshaken.

⁸ Your hand will unmask all your enemies,
your right hand all who hate you;
⁹ you will make them like a blazing furnace,
the day that you appear,^b
Yahweh will engulf them in his anger,
and fire will devour them;
¹⁰ you will wipe their children from the earth,
their descendants from among the sons of men.

¹¹ Plot though they do to harm you
and weave their plan as they may, they cannot win;
¹² since you will make them turn tail,
by shooting your arrows in their faces.

¹³ Rise, Yahweh, in your power!
We will sing and play in honor of your strength.

PSALM 22   V 21

The sufferings and hope of the virtuous man^a

*For the choirmaster – To the "Doe of the Dawn"^b –
Psalm – Of David*

¹ My God, my God, why have you deserted me?
How far from saving me, the words I groan!

2 I call all day, my God, but you never answer,
   all night long I call and cannot rest.
3 Yet, Holy One, you
   who make your home in the praises of Israel,[c]
4 in you our fathers put their trust,
   they trusted and you rescued them;
5 they called to you for help and they were saved,
   they never trusted you in vain.

6 Yet here am I, now more worm than man,
   scorn of mankind, jest of the people,
7 all who see me jeer at me,
   they toss their heads and sneer,
8 "He relied on[d] Yahweh, let Yahweh save him!
   If Yahweh is his friend, let Him rescue him!"

9 Yet you drew me out of the womb,
   you entrusted me to my mother's breasts;
10 placed on your lap from my birth,
   from my mother's womb you have been my God.
11 Do not stand aside: trouble is near,
   I have no one to help me!

12 A herd of bulls surrounds me,
   strong bulls of Bashan close in on me;
13 their jaws are agape for me,
   like lions tearing and roaring.

14 I am like water draining away,
   my bones are all disjointed,
   my heart is like wax,
   melting inside me;
15a my palate[e] is drier than a potsherd
15b and my tongue is stuck to my jaw.

16 A pack of dogs surrounds me,
   a gang of villains closes me in;
   they tie me[f] hand and foot
15c and leave me[g] lying in the dust of death.

43

¹⁷ I can count^h every one of my bones,
and there they glare at me, gloating;
¹⁸ they divide my garments among them
and cast lots for my clothes.

¹⁹ Do not stand aside, Yahweh.
O my strength, come quickly to my help;
²⁰ rescue my soul from the sword,
my dear life from the paw of the dog,
²¹ save me from the lion's mouth,
my poor soulⁱ from the wild bulls' horns!

²² Then I shall proclaim your name to my brothers,
praise you in full assembly:
²³ you who fear Yahweh, praise him!
Entire race of Jacob, glorify him!
Entire race of Israel, revere him!

²⁴ For he has not despised
or disdained the poor man in his poverty,
has not hidden his face from him,
but has answered him when he called.

²⁵ You are the theme of my praise in the Great Assembly,
I perform my vows in the presence of those who fear
him.
²⁶ The poor will receive as much as they want to eat.^j
Those who seek Yahweh will praise him.
Long life to their hearts!^k

²⁷ The whole earth, from end to end, will remember and
come back to Yahweh;
all the families of the nations will bow down before
him.^l
²⁸ For Yahweh reigns, the ruler of nations!
²⁹ Before him^m all the prosperous of the earth will bow
down,
before him will bow all who go down to the dust.
³⁰ And my soul will live for him, my children will serve
him;

31 men will proclaim the Lord to generations still to
      come,[n]
   his righteousness to a people yet unborn. All this he has
   done.[o]

PSALM 23   V 22

The Good Shepherd[a]

Psalm — Of David

1 Yahweh is my shepherd,
     I lack nothing.
2 In meadows of green grass he lets me lie.
   To the waters of repose he leads me;
3   there he revives my soul.

   He guides me by paths of virtue
     for the sake of his name.

4 Though I pass through a gloomy valley,
     I fear no harm;
   beside me[b] your rod and your staff
     are there, to hearten me.

5 You prepare a table before me
     under the eyes of my enemies;
   you anoint my head with oil,[c]
     my cup brims over.

6 Ah, how goodness and kindness pursue me,
     every day of my life;
   my home,[d] the house of Yahweh,
     as long as I live!

Antiphonal psalm for solemn entry into the sanctuary[a]

Psalm – Of David

1 To Yahweh belong earth and all it holds,
the world and all who live in it;
2 he himself founded it on the ocean,
based it firmly on the nether sea.[b]

3 Who has the right to climb the mountain of Yahweh,
who the right to stand in his holy place?
4 He whose hands are clean, whose heart is pure,
whose soul does not pay homage to worthless things
and who never swears to a lie.

5 The blessing of Yahweh is his,
and vindication from God his savior.
6 Such are the people who seek him,
who seek your presence, God of Jacob![c]   *Pause*

7 Gates, raise your arches,
rise, you ancient doors,
let the king of glory in!

8 Who is this king of glory?
Yahweh the strong, the valiant,
Yahweh valiant in battle!

9 Gates, raise your arches,
rise, you ancient doors,
let the king of glory in!

10 Who is this king of glory?
He is Yahweh Sabaoth,
King of glory, he!   *Pause*

PSALM 25

Prayer in danger

Of David

1 *Aleph* To you, Yahweh, I lift up my soul,
2 O my God.

Beth I rely on you, do not let me be shamed,
do not let my enemies gloat over me!
3 *Ghimel* No, those who hope in you are never shamed,
shame awaits disappointed traitors.

4 *Daleth* Yahweh, make your ways known to me,
teach me your paths.
5 *He* Set me in the way of your truth, and teach me,
for you are the God who saves me.

Waw All day long I hope in you
7c because of your goodness, Yahweh.
6 *Zain* Remember your kindness, Yahweh,
your love, that you showed long ago.
7a *Heth* Do not remember the sins of my youth;
7b but rather, with your love remember me.

8 *Teth* Yahweh is so good, so upright,
he teaches the way to sinners;
9 *Yod* in all that is right he guides the humble,
and instructs the poor in his way.

10 *Kaph* All Yahweh's paths are love and truth
for those who keep his covenant and his decrees.
11 *Lamed* For the sake of your name, Yahweh,
forgive my guilt, for it is great.

12 *Mem* Everyone who fears Yahweh
 will be taught the course a man should choose;
13 *Nun* his soul will live in prosperity,
 his children have the land for their own.[a]
14 *Samek* The close secret of Yahweh[b] belongs to them
 who fear him,
 his covenant also, to bring them knowledge.

15 *Ain* My eyes are always on Yahweh,
 for he releases my feet from the net.
16 *Pe* Turn to me, take pity on me,
 alone and wretched as I am!

17 *Sade* Relieve[c] the distress of my heart,
 free me from my sufferings.
18 *Qoph* See my misery and pain,
 forgive all my sins!

19 *Resh* See how my enemies multiply,
 and how violent their hatred has grown.
20 *Shin* Watch over my soul, rescue me;
 let me not be shamed: I take shelter in you.
21 *Tau* Let innocence and integrity be my protection,
 since my hope is in you, Yahweh.

Redeem Israel, God,
from all his troubles.

PSALM 26   V 25

Prayer of the blameless[a]

Of David

1 Yahweh, be my judge!
 I go my way in my innocence,
 My trust in Yahweh never wavers.

2 Test me, Yahweh, and probe me,
  put me to the trial, loins and heart;
3 for your love is before my eyes,
  and I live my life in loyalty to you.

4 No sitting with wastrels for me,
  no associating with hypocrites;
5 I hate the society of evil men,
  I refuse to sit down with the wicked.

6 I wash my hands in innocence
  and join the procession round your altar,[b]
7 singing a hymn of thanksgiving,
  proclaiming all your wonders.
8 I love the house where you live,[c]
  the place where your glory makes its home.

9 Do not let my soul share the fate of sinners,
  or my life the doom of men of blood,
10 men with guilt on their hands,
  whose right hands are heavy with bribes.

11 But I live my life in innocence,
  redeem me, Yahweh,[d] take pity on me;
12 my foot is set on the right path,
  I bless you, Yahweh, at the Assemblies.[e]

PSALM 27   V 26

In God's company there is no fear

Of David

1 Yahweh is my light and my salvation,
  whom need I fear?
  Yahweh is the fortress of my life,
  of whom should I be afraid?

2　　When evil men advance against me
　　　　to devour my flesh,
　　they, my opponents, my enemies,
　　　　are the ones who stumble and fall.

3　　Though an army pitched camp against me,
　　　　my heart would not fear;
　　though war were waged against me,
　　　　my trust would still be firm.

4　　One thing I ask of Yahweh,
　　　　one thing I seek:
　　to live in the house of Yahweh
　　　　all the days of my life,
　　to enjoy the sweetness of Yahweh
　　　　and to consult him in his Temple.

5　　For he shelters me under his awning
　　　　in times of trouble;
　　he hides me deep in his tent,[a]
　　　　sets me high on a rock.

6　　And now my head is held high
　　　　over the enemies who surround me,
　　in his tent I will offer
　　　　exultant sacrifice.

　　I will sing, I will play for Yahweh!

7　　Yahweh, hear my voice as I cry!
　　　　Pity me! Answer me!
8　　My heart has said of you,
　　　　"Seek his face."[b]
　　Yahweh, I do seek your face;
9　　　　do not hide your face from me.

　　Do not repulse your servant in anger;
　　　　you are my help.
　　Never leave me, never desert me,
　　　　God, my savior!
10　If my father and mother desert me,
　　　　Yahweh will care for me still.

11 Yahweh, teach me your way,
   lead me in the path of integrity
      because of my enemies;
12 do not abandon me to the will of my foes—
   false witnesses have risen against me,
      and breathe out violence.

13 This I believe: I shall see[c] the goodness of Yahweh,
   in the land of the living.
14 Put your hope in Yahweh, be strong, let your heart be
      bold,
   put your hope in Yahweh.

PSALM 28   V 27

Petition and thanksgiving

Of David

1 I cry for you, Yahweh,
   my Rock! Do not be deaf to me,
   for if you are silent, I shall go
      down to the Pit like the rest.

2 Hear my voice, raised in petition,
   as I cry to you for help,
   as I raise my hands, Yahweh,[a]
      toward your Holy of Holies.

3 Do not drag me away with the wicked,
   away with the evil men
   who talk of peace to their neighbors
      while malice is in their hearts.

4 Repay them for their actions, Yahweh,
   for the evil they commit,
   for their handiwork repay them,
      let them have what they deserve!

51

⁵ How blind they are to the works of Yahweh,
to his own handiwork!
May he pull them down and not rebuild them!

⁶ Blessed be Yahweh, for he hears
the sound of my petition!

⁷ Yahweh is my strength, my shield,
my heart puts its trust in him;
I have been helped, my flesh has bloomed again,[b]
I thank him with all my heart.

⁸ Yahweh is the strength of his people,
a saving fortress for his anointed.[c]
⁹ Save your people! Bless your heritage!
Shepherd them; carry them for ever!

PSALM 29   V 28

Hymn to the lord of the storm[a]

Psalm – Of David

¹ Pay tribute to Yahweh, you sons of God,[b]
tribute to Yahweh of glory and power,
² tribute to Yahweh of the glory of his name,
worship Yahweh in his sacred court.[c]

³ᵃ The voice of Yahweh over the waters!
³ᶜ Yahweh over the multitudinous waters!
⁴ The voice of Yahweh in power!
The voice of Yahweh in splendor!

⁵ The voice of Yahweh shatters the cedars,
Yahweh shatters the cedars of Lebanon,
⁶ making Lebanon leap like a calf,
Sirion[d] like a young wild bull.

⁷ The voice of Yahweh sharpens lightning shafts!^e

⁸ The voice of Yahweh sets the wilderness shaking.
Yahweh shakes the wilderness of Kadesh.
^{9a} The voice of Yahweh sets the terebinths^f shuddering,
^{9b} stripping the forests bare.

^{3b} The God of glory thunders.
^{9c} In his palace^g everything cries, "Glory!"
¹⁰ Yahweh sat enthroned for the Blood,
Yahweh sits enthroned as a king for ever.^h

¹¹ Yahweh gives strength to his people,
Yahweh blesses his people with peace.

PSALM 30   V 29

Thanksgiving after mortal danger

Psalm – Canticle for the Dedication of the House – Of David

¹ High praise, Yahweh, I give you, for you have helped
me up,
and not let my enemies gloat over me.
² Yahweh, my God, I cried to you for help, and you
have healed me.
³ Yahweh, you have brought my soul up from Sheol,
of all those who go down to the Pit you have revived me.

⁴ Play music in Yahweh's honor, you devout,
remember his holiness, and praise him.
⁵ His anger lasts a moment, his favor a lifetime;
in the evening, a spell of tears,^a in the morning, shouts
of joy.

⁶ In my prosperity, I used to say,
"Nothing can ever shake me!"

7   Your favor, Yahweh, stood me on a peak impregnable;[b]
    but then you hid your face and I was terrified.

8   Yahweh, I call to you,
        I beg my God[c] to pity me,
9   "What do you gain by my blood[d] if I go down to the Pit?
    Can the dust praise you or proclaim your faithfulness?

10   "Hear, Yahweh, take pity on me;
        Yahweh, help me!"
11 You have turned my mourning into dancing,
    you have stripped off my sackcloth and wrapped me in
        gladness;
12 and now my heart, silent no longer, will play you music;
    Yahweh, my God, I will praise you for ever.

PSALM 31   V 30

Prayer in time of ordeal

For the choirmaster – Psalm – Of David

1   In you, Yahweh, I take shelter;
    never let me be disgraced.
    In your righteousness deliver me, rescue me,[a]
2   turn your ear to me, make haste!

    Be a sheltering rock for me,
    a walled fortress to save me!
3   For you are my rock, my fortress;
    for the sake of your name, guide me, lead me!

4   Pull me out of the net they have spread for me,
    for you are my refuge;
5   into your hands I commit my spirit,
    you have redeemed me, Yahweh.

6 God of truth, you hate[b]
   those who serve worthless idols;
   but I put my trust in Yahweh:
7 I will exult, and rejoice in your love!

   You, who have seen my wretchedness,
   and known the miseries of my soul,
8 have not handed me over to the enemy,
   you have given my feet space and to spare.

9 Take pity on me, Yahweh,
   I am in trouble now.
   Grief wastes away my eye,
   my throat, my inmost parts.

10 For my life is worn out with sorrow,
   my years with sighs;
   my strength yields under misery,[c]
   my bones are wasting away.

11 To every one of my oppressors
   I am contemptible,
   loathsome[d] to my neighbors,
   to my friends a thing of fear.

   Those who see me in the street
   hurry past me;
12 I am forgotten, as good as dead in their hearts,
   something discarded.

13 I hear their endless slanders,
   threats from every quarter,
   as they combine against me,
   plotting to take my life.

14 But I put my trust in you, Yahweh,
   I say, "You are my God."
15 My days are in your hand, rescue me
   from the hands of my enemies and persecutors;
16 let your face smile on your servant,
   save me in your love.

55

17   I invoke you, Yahweh; do not let me be disgraced,
         let the disgrace fall on the wicked!
     May they go speechless to Sheol,
18   their lying lips struck dumb
     for those insolent slurs on the virtuous,
         for that arrogance and contempt.

19   Yahweh,*e* how great your goodness,
         reserved for those who fear you,
     bestowed on those who take shelter in you,
         for all mankind to see!

20   Safe in your presence you hide them
         far from the wiles of men;
     inside your tent you shelter them
         far from the war of tongues.*f*

21   Blessed be Yahweh, who performs
         marvels of love for me
         (in a fortress-city)!
22   In my alarm I exclaimed,
         "I have been snatched*g* out of your sight!"
     Yet you heard my petition
         when I called to you for help.

23   Love Yahweh, all you devout:
         Yahweh, protector of the faithful,
     will repay the arrogant
         with interest.
24   Be strong, let your heart be bold,
         all you who hope in Yahweh!

Candid admission of sin[a]

Of David – Poem

1 Happy the man whose fault is forgiven,
    whose sin is blotted out;[b]
2 happy the man whom Yahweh
    accuses of no guilt,
  whose spirit is incapable of deceit!

3 All the time I kept silent, my bones were wasting away
    with groans, day in, day out;
4 day and night your hand
    lay heavy on me;
  my heart grew parched as stubble[c]
    in summer drought.   *Pause*

5 At last I admitted to you I had sinned;
    no longer concealing my guilt,
  I said, "I will go to Yahweh
    and confess my fault."
  And you, you have forgiven the wrong I did,
    have pardoned[d] my sin.   *Pause*

6 That is why each of your servants prays to you
    in time of trouble;[e]
  even if floods come rushing down,
    they will never reach him.
7 You are a hiding place for me,
    you guard me when in trouble,
  you surround me with songs[f] of deliverance.   *Pause*

8 I will instruct you, and teach you the way to go;
  I will watch over you and be your adviser.

9   Do not be like senseless horse or mule
    that need bit and bridle to curb their spirit[g]
    (to let you get near them).

10 Many torments await the wicked,
    but grace enfolds the man who trusts in Yahweh.

11   Rejoice in Yahweh,
        exult, you virtuous,
        shout for joy, all upright hearts.

PSALM 33   V 32

Hymn to Providence

1   Shout for joy to Yahweh, all virtuous men,
    praise comes well from upright hearts;
2   give thanks to Yahweh on the lyre,
    play to him on the ten-string harp;
3   sing a new song in his honor,
    play with all your skill as you acclaim[a] him!
4   The word of Yahweh is integrity itself,
    all he does is done faithfully;
5   he loves virtue and justice,
    Yahweh's love fills the earth.

6   By the word of Yahweh the heavens were made,
    their whole array by the breath of his mouth;
7   he collects the ocean waters as though in a wineskin,[b]
    he stores the deeps in cellars.

8   Let the whole world fear Yahweh,
    let all who live on earth revere him!
9   He spoke, and it was created;
    he commanded, and there it stood.

10 Yahweh thwarts the plans of nations,
    frustrates the intentions of peoples;
11 but Yahweh's plans hold good for ever,
    the intentions of his heart from age to age.
12 Happy the nation whose God is Yahweh,
    the people he has chosen for his heritage.

13 Yahweh looks down from heaven,
    he sees the whole human race;
14 from where he sits he watches
    all who live on the earth,
15 he who molds every heart
    and takes note of all men do.

16 A large army will not keep a king safe,
    nor does the hero escape by his great strength;
17 it is delusion to rely on the horse for safety,
    for all its power, it cannot save.

18 But see how the eye of Yahweh is on those who fear him,
    on those who rely on his love,
19 to rescue their souls from death
    and keep them alive in famine.

20 Our soul awaits Yahweh,
    he is our help and shield;
21 our hearts rejoice in him,
    we trust in his holy name.
22 Yahweh, let your love rest on us
    as our hope has rested in you.

In praise of God's justice[a]

Of David. When, after pretending to be mad in front of Abimelech, he was dismissed by him and made his escape

1 *Aleph* I will bless Yahweh at all times,
   his praise shall be on my lips continually;
2 *Beth* my soul glories in Yahweh,
   let the humble hear and rejoice.

3 *Ghimel* Proclaim with me the greatness of Yahweh,
   together let us extol his name.
4 *Daleth* I seek Yahweh, and he answers me
   and frees me from all my fears.

5 *He* Every face turned to him grows brighter
   and is never ashamed.
6 *Zain* A cry goes up from the poor man, and Yahweh
      hears,
   and helps him in all his troubles.

7 *Heth* The angel of Yahweh pitches camp
   round those who fear him; and he keeps them safe.
8 *Teth* How good Yahweh is—only taste and see!
   Happy the man who takes shelter in him.

9 *Yod* Fear Yahweh, you his holy ones:
   those who fear him want for nothing.
10 *Kaph* The young lion[b] may go empty and hungry,
   but those who seek Yahweh lack nothing good.

11 *Lamed* Come, my sons, listen to me,
   I will teach you the fear of Yahweh.
12 *Mem* Which of you wants to live to the full,
   who loves long life and enjoyment of prosperity?

13 *Nun*   Malice must be banished from your tongue,
deceitful conversation from your lips;
14 *Samek*   never yield to evil, practice good,
seek peace, pursue it.

16 *Pe*   The face of Yahweh frowns on evil men,
to wipe their memory from the earth;
15 *Ain*   the eyes of Yahweh are turned toward the virtuous,
his ears to their cry.

17 *Sade*   They cry for help and Yahweh hears
and rescues them from all their troubles;
18 *Qoph*   Yahweh is near to the brokenhearted,
he helps those whose spirit is crushed.

19 *Resh*   Hardships in plenty beset the virtuous man,
but Yahweh rescues him from them all;
20 *Shin*   taking care of every bone,
Yahweh will not let one be broken.

21 *Tau*   Evil will bring death to the wicked,[c]
those who hate the virtuous will have to pay;
22 (*Waw*)   while Yahweh himself ransoms the souls of his
servants,
and those who take shelter in him have nothing to pay.

PSALM 35   V 34

Prayer of a virtuous man under oppression[a]

Of David

1 Accuse my accusers, Yahweh,
attack my attackers;
2 grip shield and buckler,
up, and help me;

³ brandish lance and pike[b]
   in the faces of my pursuers.
   Tell my soul, "I am your salvation."

⁴ Shame and dishonor on those
   who are out to kill me!
   Back with them! Cover with confusion
   those who plot my downfall!
⁵ May they be like chaff before the wind,
   with the angel of Yahweh to chase them!
⁶ May their way be dark and slippery,
   with the angel of Yahweh to hound them!

⁷ Unprovoked they spread their net for me,
   they dug a pit[c] for me;
⁸ but Ruin creeps on them unawares,
   the net they have spread will catch them instead,
   and into their own pit will they fall.

⁹ Then my soul will rejoice in Yahweh,
   exult that he has saved me.
¹⁰ All my bones will exclaim, "Yahweh,
   who can compare with you
   in rescuing the poor man from the stronger,
   the needy from the man who exploits him?"

¹¹ Lying witnesses take the stand,
   questioning me on things I know nothing about;
¹² they repay my kindness with evil,
   there is desolation in my soul.

¹³ Yet, when they were sick, I put sackcloth on,
   I humbled my soul with fasting,
   murmuring prayers to my own breast
¹⁴   as though for a friend or brother;
   and, like a person mourning his mother,
   went about dejected and sorrowing.

¹⁵ Now I have fallen, they crowd round delighted,
   flocking to jeer at me;

strangers[d] I never even knew
    with loud cries tear me to pieces,
16 riddling me with gibe after gibe,[e]
    grinding their teeth at me.

17 How much longer, Lord, will you look on?
    Rescue my soul from their onslaughts,[f]
    my dear life from these lions.
18 I will give thanks in the Great Assembly,
    praise you where the people throng.

19 Do not let my lying enemies
    gloat over me,
do not let those who hate me for no reason
    exchange sly glances.

20 Peace is not what they discuss
    with the[g] peace-loving people of the land;
they think out false accusations,
21   their mouths wide to accuse me,
"Aha! Aha!" they say
    "With our own eyes we saw it!"[h]

22 Now break your silence, Yahweh, you were looking too,
    Lord, do not stand aside,
23 up, wake up, come to my defense,
    Lord my God side with me!
24 Yahweh my God, you are righteous, so give verdict for
    me,
    and do not let them gloat over me.

25 Do not let them think, "Just as we hoped!"
    Do not let them say, "Now we have got him down!"
26 Shame and dishonor on all
    who gloat over my misfortune;
shame and discredit cover all
    who profit at my expense!

27 But shouts of joy and gladness for all
    who take pleasure in my virtue;

give them constant cause to say,
   "Great is Yahweh,
who likes to see his servant at peace!"

28 Then my tongue will shout your goodness,
   and sing your praises all day long.

PSALM 36

The wickedness of the sinner, the goodness of God[a]

For the choirmaster – Of the servant of Yahweh, David

1 The wicked man's oracle is Sin
   in the depths of his heart;[b]
   there is no fear of God
   before his eyes.

2 He sees himself with too flattering an eye
   to detect and detest his guilt;[c]
3 all he says tends to mischief and deceit,
   he has turned his back on wisdom.

4 How best to work mischief he plots,
   even when he is in bed;
   he persists in his evil course,
   he never rejects what is bad.

5 Your love, Yahweh, reaches to the heavens,
   your faithfulness to the clouds;
6 your righteousness is like the mountains of God,[d]
   your judgments like the mighty deep.

   Yahweh, protector of man and beast,
7 how precious, God, your love!
   Hence the sons of men
   take shelter in the shadow of your wings.[e]

8 They feast on the bounty of your house,
   you give them drink from your river of pleasure;
9 yes, with you is the fountain of life,[f]
   by your light we see the light.[g]

10 Do not stop loving those who know you,
    or being righteous to upright hearts.
11 Do not let arrogant feet crush me
    or wicked hands expel me.

12 The evil men have fallen, there they lie,
    beaten down, never to stand again!

PSALM 37

The fate of the virtuous and the wicked[a]

Of David

1 *Aleph* Do not worry about the wicked,
   do not envy those who do wrong.
2 Quick as the grass they wither,
   fading like the green in the field.

3 *Beth* Trust in Yahweh and do what is good,
   make your home in the land[b] and live in peace;
4 make Yahweh your only joy
   and he will give you what your heart desires.

5 *Ghimel* Commit your fate to Yahweh,
   trust in him and he will act:
6 making your virtue clear as the light,
   your integrity as bright as noon.

7 *Daleth* Be quiet before Yahweh, and wait patiently
      for him,
   not worrying about men who make their fortunes,
   about men who scheme
14c to bring the poor and needy down.

⁸ *He* Enough of anger, leave rage aside,
do not worry, nothing but evil can come of it:
⁹ for the wicked will be expelled,
while those who hope in Yahweh shall have the land for
their own.

¹⁰ *Waw* A little longer, and the wicked will be no more,
search his place well, he will not be there;
¹¹ but the humble shall have the land for their own
to enjoy untroubled peace.

¹² *Zain* The wicked man plots against the virtuous,
and grinds his teeth at him;
¹³ but the Lord only laughs at the man,
knowing his end is in sight.

¹⁴ᵃ *Heth* Though the wicked draw the sword,
¹⁴ᵇ and bend their bow, to kill the upright,
¹⁵ their swords will only pierce their own hearts
and their bows will be smashed.

¹⁶ *Teth* The little the virtuous possesses
outweighs all the wealth of the wicked,ᶜ
¹⁷ since the arms of the wicked are doomed to break,
and Yahweh will uphold the virtuous.

¹⁸ *Yod* Yahweh takes care of good men's lives,
and their heritage will last for ever;
¹⁹ they will not be at a loss when bad times come,
in time of famine they will have more than they need.

²⁰ *Kaph* As for the wicked—they will perish,
these enemies of Yahweh;
they will vanish like the beauty of the meadows,
they will vanish in smoke.

²¹ *Lamed* The wicked man borrows without meaning to
repay,
but a virtuous man is generous and openhanded;
²² those he blesses will have the land for their own,
those he cursesᵈ will be expelled.

23 *Mem* Yahweh guides a man's steps,
they are sure, and he takes pleasure in his progress;
24 he may fall, but never fatally,
since Yahweh supports him by the hand.

25 *Nun* Now I am old, but ever since my youth
I never saw a virtuous man deserted,
or his descendants forced to beg their bread;
26 he is always compassionate, always lending:
his children will be blessed.

27 *Samek* Never yield to evil, practice good
and you will have an everlasting home,
28 for Yahweh loves what is right,
and never deserts the devout.

Ain Those who do wrong[e] will perish once and for all,
and the children of the wicked shall be expelled;
29 the virtuous will have the land for their own,
and make it their home for ever.

30 *Pe* The mouth of the virtuous man murmurs wisdom,
and his tongue speaks what is right;
31 with the Law of his God in his heart
his steps can never falter.

32 *Sade* The wicked man spies on the virtuous,
seeking to kill him;
33 Yahweh will never leave him in those clutches,
or let him be condemned under trial.

34a *Qoph* Put your hope in Yahweh, keep his way,
40b and he will save you from the wicked,
34b raising you until you make the land your own
and see the wicked expelled.

35 *Resh* I have seen the wicked in his triumph
towering like a cedar of Lebanon,[f]
36 but when next I passed,[g] he was not there,
I looked for him and he was nowhere to be found.

[37] *Shin* Observe the innocent man, consider the upright:
for the man of peace there are descendants,
[38] but sinners shall be destroyed altogether,
the descendants of the wicked shall be wiped out.

[39] *Tau* The salvation of the virtuous comes from Yahweh,
he is their shelter when trouble comes;
[40a] Yahweh helps and rescues them,
he saves them because they take shelter in him.

PSALM 38   V 37
Prayer in distress[a]

Psalm – Of David – In commemoration

[1] Yahweh, do not punish me in your rage,
or reprove me in the heat of anger.
[2] Your arrows have pierced deep,
your hand has pressed down[b] on me;
[3] no soundness in my flesh now you are angry,
no health in my bones, because of my sin.

[4] My guilt is overwhelming me,
it is too heavy a burden;
[5] my wounds stink and are festering,
the result of my folly;
[6] bowed down, bent double, overcome,
I go mourning all the day.

[7] My loins are burnt up with fever,
there is no soundness in my flesh:
[8] numbed and crushed and overcome,
my heart groans, I moan aloud.

[9] Lord, all that I long for is known to you,
my sighing is no secret from you;

10 my heart is throbbing, my strength deserting me,
    the light of my eyes itself has left me.

11 My friends and my companions shrink from my wounds,
    even the dearest of them keep their distance;
12 men intent on killing me lay snares,
    others, hoping to hurt me, threaten my ruin,
    hatching treacherous plots all day.

13 But I am like the deaf, I do not hear,
    like the dumb man who does not open his mouth;
14 I am like the man who, hearing nothing,
    gives no sharp answer in return.

15 For I put my trust in you, Yahweh,
    and leave you to answer for me, Lord my God.
16 I have already said, "Stop them gloating over me,
    do not let them take advantage of me if my foot should
       slip."

17 And now my fall is upon me,
    there is no relief from my pains;
18 yes, I admit my guilt,
    I am sorry for having sinned.

19 There are more and more to hurt me for no reason,[o]
    There are more to hate me unprovoked,
20 Repaying my kindness with evil,
    arraigning me for trying to do right.[d]

21 Yahweh, do not desert me,
    do not stand aside, my God!
22 Come quickly to my help,
    Lord, my savior!

The insignificance of man before God[a]

For the choirmaster – For Jeduthun – Psalm – Of David

1　I said, "I will watch how I behave,
　　and not let my tongue lead me into sin;
　　I will keep a muzzle on my mouth
　　as long as the wicked man is near me."
2　I stayed dumb, silent, speechless,
　　though the sight of him thriving[b] made torment increase.

3　My heart had been smoldering inside me,
　　but it flared up at the thought of this
　　and the words burst out,
4　"Tell me, Yahweh, when my end will be,
　　how many days are allowed me,
　　show me how frail I am.

5　"Look, you have given me an inch or two of life,
　　my life-span is nothing to you;
　　each man that stands on earth is only a puff of wind,
　　　　　　　　　　　　　　　　　　　　Pause

6　every man that walks, only a shadow,
　　and the wealth[c] he amasses is only a puff of wind—
　　he does not know who will take it next."

7　So tell me, Lord, what can I expect?
　　My hope is in you.
8　Free me from all my sins,
　　do not make me the butt of idiots.
9　I am dumb, I speak no more,
　　since you yourself have been at work.

¹⁰ Lay your scourge aside,
I am worn out with the blows you deal me.
¹¹ You punish man with the penalties of sin,
like a moth you eat away all that gives him pleasure—
man is indeed only a puff of wind!   *Pause*

¹² Yahweh, hear my prayer,
listen to my cry for help,
do not stay deaf to my crying.
I am your guest, and only for a time,
a nomad like all my ancestors.
¹³ Look away, let me draw breath,[d]
before I go away and am no more!

PSALM 40   V 39

Song of praise and prayer for help[a]

For the choirmaster – Psalm – Of David

¹ I waited and waited for Yahweh,
now at last he has stooped to me
and heard my cry for help.

² He has pulled me out of the horrible pit,
out of the slough of the marsh,
has settled my feet on a rock
and steadied my steps.

³ He has put a new song in my mouth,
a song of praise to our God;
dread will seize many at the sight,
and they will put their trust in Yahweh.

⁴ Happy the man who puts
his trust in Yahweh,
and does not side with rebels
who stray after false gods.

5 How many wonders you have done for us,
     Yahweh, my God!
   How many plans you have made for us;
     you have no equal!
   I want to proclaim them, again and again,
     but they are more than I can count.

6 You, who wanted no sacrifice or oblation,
     opened[b] my ear,
   you asked no holocaust or sacrifice for sin;
7   then I said, "Here I am! I am coming!"

   In the scroll of the book am I not commanded
8   to obey your will?[c]
   My God, I have always loved your Law
     from the depths of my being.

9 I have always proclaimed the righteousness of Yahweh
     in the Great Assembly;
   nor do I mean to stop proclaiming,
     as you know well.

10 I have never kept your righteousness to myself,
     but have spoken of your faithfulness and saving help;
   I have made no secret of your love and faithfulness
     in the Great Assembly.

11 For your part, Yahweh, do not withhold
     your kindness from me!
   May your love and faithfulness
     constantly preserve me.

12 More misfortunes beset me
     than I can count,
   my sins close in on me
     until I can hardly see,
   they outnumber the hairs on my head;
     my courage is running out.

13 Oh come and rescue me, Yahweh,
   Yahweh come quickly and help me!

¹⁴ Shame and dishonor on all
who are out to kill, to destroy me!

Down with them! Disgrace on those
who enjoy my misfortune!
¹⁵ May they be aghast with shame,
those who say to me, "Aha! Aha!"

¹⁶ But joy and gladness
for all who seek you!
To all who love your saving power
give constant cause to say, "God is great!"

¹⁷ To me, poor wretch,
come quickly, Lord![a]
My helper, my savior, my God,
come and do not delay!

PSALM 41   V 40

Prayer of a sick and lonely man

For the choirmaster – Psalm – Of David

¹ Happy the man who cares for the poor[a] and the weak:
if disaster strikes, Yahweh will come to his help.
² Yahweh will guard him, give life and happiness[b] in the
land;
ah, do not let his enemies treat him as they please!
³ Yahweh will be his comfort on his bed of sickness;
most carefully you make his bed[c] when he is sick.

⁴ I for my part said, "Yahweh, take pity on me!
Cure me, for I have sinned against you."
⁵ My enemies say of me with malice,
"How long before he dies and his name perishes?"
⁶ They visit me, their hearts full of spite,
they offer hollow comfort, and go out to spread the news.

⁷ All who hate me whisper to each other about me,
 reckoning I deserve the misery I suffer,[d]
⁸ "This sickness is fatal[e] that has overtaken him,
 he is down at last, he will never get up again."
⁹ Even my closest and most trusted friend,
 who shared my table, rebels[f] against me.

¹⁰ But Yahweh, take pity on me!
 Raise me up, and I will pay them back;
¹¹ and by this I shall know that I enjoy your favor,
 if my enemy fails to triumph over me;
¹² and I, whom you uphold, go unscathed,
 set by you in your presence for ever.
¹³ Blessed be Yahweh, the God of Israel,
 from all eternity and for ever!
 Amen. Amen![g]

PSALM 42–43   V 41–42

Lament of a Levite in exile[a]

For the choirmaster – Poem – Of the sons of Korah

¹ As a doe[b] longs
 for running streams,
 so longs my soul
 for you, my God.

² My soul thirsts for God,
 the God of life;
 when shall I go to see
 the face of God?[c]

³ I have no food but tears,
 day and night;
 and all day long men say to me,
 "Where is your God?"

⁴ I remember, and my soul
 melts within me:
I am on my way to the wonderful Tent,^d
 to the house of God,
among cries of joy and praise
 and an exultant throng.

⁵ Why so downcast, my soul,
 why do you sigh within me?
Put your hope in God: I shall praise him yet,
⁶ my savior,^e my God.

When my soul is downcast within me,
 I think of you;
from the land of Jordan and of Hermon,
 of you, humble mountain!^f

⁷ Deep is calling to deep
 as your cataracts roar;
all your waves, your breakers,
 have rolled over me.

⁸ In the daytime may Yahweh
 command his love to come,
and by night may his song be on my lips,
 a prayer to the God of my life!

⁹ Let me say to God my Rock,
 "Why do you forget me?
Why must I walk
 so mournfully, oppressed by the enemy?"

¹⁰ Nearly breaking my bones^g
 my oppressors insult me,
as all day long they ask me,
 "Where is your God?"

¹¹ Why so downcast, my soul,
 why do you sigh within me?
Put your hope in God: I shall praise him yet,
 my savior, my God.

43

1 Defend me,[a] take up my cause
    against people who have no pity;
from the treacherous and cunning man
    rescue me, God.

2 It is you, God, who are my shelter:
    why do you abandon me?
Why must I walk
    so mournfully, oppressed by the enemy?

3 Send out your light and your truth,
    let these be my guide,
to lead me to your holy mountain
    and to the place where you live.

4 Then I shall go to the altar of God,
    to the God of my joy,[b]
I shall rejoice, I shall praise you on the harp,
    Yahweh, my God.

5 Why so downcast, my soul,
    why do you sigh within me?
Put your hope in God: I shall praise him yet,
    my savior, my God.

PSALM 44   V 43

National lament[a]

For the choirmaster – Of the sons of Korah – Psalm

1 God, we have heard with our own ears,
    our ancestors have told us
of the deeds you performed in their days,
2 in days long ago, by your hand.[b]

To put them in the land you dispossessed the nations,
you harried the peoples to make room for them;
3 it was not by their swords they won the land,
it was not by their arms they gained the victory:
it was your right hand, your arm
and the light of your face—because you loved them.

4 You it was, my King, my God,
who won those victories for Jacob;
5 through you we trampled down our enemies,
through your name we subdued our aggressors.

6 My trust was not in my bow,
my sword did not gain me victory:
7 we conquered our enemies through you,
you, who defeated all who hated us—
8 our boast was always of God,
we praised your name without ceasing.   *Pause*

9 Yet now you abandon and scorn us,
you no longer march with our armies,
10 you allow the enemy to push us back,
and let those who hate us raid us when it suits them.

11 You let us go to the slaughterhouse like sheep,
you scatter us among the nations;
12 you sell your people for next to nothing,
and make no profit from the bargain.

13 Thanks to you, our neighbors insult us,
all those around us make us their butt and laughingstock;
14 you make us a byword to pagans,
a thing to make them toss their heathen heads.*c*

15 All day long I brood on this disgrace,
my face covered in shame,
16 under a shower of insult and blasphemy,
a display of hatred and revenge.

17 All this happened to us though we had not forgotten you,
though we had not been disloyal to your covenant;

77

18 though our hearts had not turned away,
   though our steps had not left your path:
19 yet you crushed us in the place where the jackals live,[d]
   and threw the shadow of death over us.

20 Had we forgotten the name of our own God
   and stretched out our hands[e] to a foreign one,
21 would not God have found this out,
   he who knows the secrets of the heart?
22 No, it is for your sake we are being massacred daily,
   and counted as sheep for the slaughter.

23 Wake up, Lord! Why are you asleep?
   Awake! Do not abandon us for good.
24 Why do you hide your face,
   and forget we are wretched and exploited?

25 For we are bowed in the dust,
   our bodies crushed to the ground.
26 Rise! Come to our help!
   Redeem us for the sake of your love.

PSALM 45   V 44
Royal wedding song[a]

*For the choirmaster – Tune: "Lilies . . ."[b] – Of the sons of
Korah – Poem – Love song*

1 My heart is stirred by a noble theme:
   I address my poem to the king;
   my tongue as ready as the pen of a busy scribe.
2 Of all men you are the most handsome,
   your lips are moist with grace,
   for God has blessed you for ever.

3 Hero, strap your sword at your side,
4 in majesty and splendor; on, ride on,
in the cause of truth, religion, and virtue!

Stretch the bowstring tight,[c]
lending terror to your right hand.
5 Your arrows are sharp; nations lie at your mercy,
the king's enemies are losing heart.

6 Your throne, God,[d] shall last for ever and ever,
your royal scepter is a scepter of integrity:
7 virtue you love as much as you hate wickedness.

This is why God, your God, has anointed you
with the oil of gladness, above all your rivals;
8 myrrh and aloes waft from[e] your robes.

From palaces of ivory harps entertain you,
9 daughters of kings are among your maids of honor;[f]
on your right stands the queen, in gold from Ophir.

10 Listen, daughter, pay careful attention:
forget your nation and your ancestral home,[g]
11 then the king will fall in love with your beauty.
He is your master now, bow down to him.

12 The daughter of Tyre will solicit your favor with gifts,
13 the wealthiest nations, with jewels set in gold.[h]

14 Dressed[i] in brocades, the king's daughter
is led in to the king, with bridesmaids in her train.

Her[j] ladies-in-waiting follow
15 and enter the king's palace to general rejoicing.

16 Your ancestors will be replaced by sons
whom you will make lords of the whole world.

17 I shall immortalize your name,
nations will sing your praises for ever and ever.

God is on our side[a]

For the choirmaster — Of the sons of Korah — For oboe — Song

1 God is our shelter, our strength,
  ever ready to help in time of trouble,
2 so we shall not be afraid when the earth gives way,
  when mountains tumble into the depths of the sea,
3 and its waters roar and seethe,
  the mountains tottering as it heaves.[b]

  (Yahweh Sabaoth is on our side,
    our citadel, the God of Jacob!)[c]   *Pause*

4 There is a river whose streams refresh the city of God,
  and it sanctifies the dwelling[d] of the Most High.
5 God is inside the city, she can never fall,
  at crack of dawn[e] God helps her;
6 to the roaring of nations and tottering of kingdoms,
  when he shouts, the world disintegrates.

7   Yahweh Sabaoth is on our side,
    our citadel, the God of Jacob!   *Pause*

8 Come, think of Yahweh's marvels,
  the astounding things he has done in the world;
9 all over the world he puts an end to wars,
  he breaks the bow, he snaps the spear,
  he gives shields[f] to the flames.
10 "Pause a while and know that I am God,
  exalted among the nations, exalted over the earth!"

11   Yahweh Sabaoth is on our side,
    our citadel, the God of Jacob!   *Pause*

PSALM 47

Yahweh, king of Israel, lord of the world[a]

For the choirmaster – Of the sons of Korah – Psalm

1 Clap your hands, all you peoples,
acclaim God with shouts of joy;
2 for Yahweh, the Most High, is to be dreaded,
the Great King of the whole world.

3 He brings the peoples under our dominion,
he puts the nations under our feet;
4 for us he chooses our heritage—
the pride of Jacob, whom he loved.

5 God rises to shouts of acclamation,
Yahweh rises to a blast of trumpets,
6 let the music sound for our[b] God, let it sound,
let the music sound for our King, let it sound!

7 God is king of the whole world:
play your best in his honor!
8 God is king of the nations,
he reigns on his holy throne.

9 The leaders of the nations rally
to the people of the God of Abraham.[c]
Every shield in the world belongs to God.
He reigns supreme.

PSALM 48

Zion, the mountain of God[a]

Song – Psalm – Of the sons of Korah

1 Yahweh is great and supremely to be praised
   in the city of our God,
2 the holy mountain, beautiful where it rises,
   joy of the whole world;

   Mount of Zion, deep heart of the North,[b]
   city of the Great King;
3 here among her palaces,
   God proved to be her fortress.

4 There was a rallying, once, of kings,
   advancing together along a common front;
5 they looked, they were amazed,
   they panicked, they ran!

6 There they shuddered and writhed
   like women in labor,
7 it was the east wind, that wrecker
   of ships of Tarshish![c]

8 What we had heard we saw for ourselves
   in the city of our God,
   the city of Yahweh Sabaoth,
   God-protected for ever.   *Pause*

9 God, in your Temple
   we reflect on your love:
10 God, your praise, like your name,
   reaches to the ends of the world.

Your right hand holds the victory;
11   Mount Zion rejoices,
the daughters of Judah[d] exult
    to have your rulings.

12   Go through Zion, walk round her,
    counting her towers,
13 admiring her walls,[e]
    reviewing her palaces;

then tell the next generation
14   that God is here,
our God and leader,[f]
    for ever and ever.

PSALM 49   V 48

The futility of riches[a]

For the choirmaster — Of the sons of Korah — Psalm

1   Hear this, all nations,
    pay attention all who live on earth,
2   important people, ordinary people,
    rich and poor alike!

3   My lips have wisdom to utter,
    my heart whispers sound sense;
4   I turn my attention to a proverb,
    and set my solution to the harp.

5   Why should I be afraid in evil times,
    when malice dogs my steps and[b] hems me in,
6   of men who trust in their wealth
    and boast of the profusion of their riches?

7 But man could never redeem himself
   or pay his ransom to God:
8 it costs so much to redeem his life,
9 it is beyond him; how then could he live on for ever
   and never see the Pit—

10 when all the time he sees that wise men die,
   that foolish and stupid perish both alike,
   and leave their fortunes to others.

11 Their tombs*º* are their eternal home,
   their lasting residence,
   though they owned estates that bore their names.

12 Man when he prospers forfeits intelligence:*ᵈ*
   he is one with the cattle doomed to slaughter.
13 So on they go with their self-assurance,
   with men to run after them when they raise their voice.*ᵉ*
                                                    Pause

14 Like sheep to be penned in Sheol,
   Death*ᶠ* will herd them to pasture
   and the upright will have the better of them.

   Dawn will come*ᵍ* and then the show they made will
        disappear,
   Sheol the home for them!
15 But God will redeem my life
   from the grasp of Sheol, and will receive me.*ʰ*   *Pause*

16 Do not be afraid when a man grows rich,
   when the glory of his House increases;
17 when he dies he can take nothing with him,
   his glory cannot follow him down.*ⁱ*

18 The soul he made so happy while he lived
   —"look after yourself and men will praise you"—
19 will join the company of his ancestors
   who will never see the light of day again.

20 Man in his prosperity forfeits intelligence:
   he is one with the cattle doomed to slaughter.

PSALM 50

Worship in spirit and truth[a]

Psalm – Of Asaph

1 Yahweh, God of gods,
  speaks, he summons the earth.
  From east to west,
2 from Zion, perfection of beauty, he shines.

3 Let our God come, and be silent no more!

  Preceding him, a devouring fire,
  round him, a raging storm;
4 he summons the heavens above
  and the earth, to his people's trial:

5 "Assemble my faithful before me
  who sealed my covenant by sacrifice!"
6 Let the heavens proclaim his righteousness
  when God himself is judge!   *Pause*

7a "Listen, my people, I am speaking;
7b Israel, I am giving evidence against you!
21c I charge, I indict you to your face,
7c I, God, your God.

8 "I am not finding fault with your sacrifices,
  those holocausts constantly before me;
9 I do not claim one extra bull from your homes,
  nor one extra goat from your pens,

10 "since all the forest animals are already mine,
   and the cattle on my mountains[b] in their thousands;
11 I know all the birds of the air,[c]
   nothing moves in the field that does not belong to me.

12 "If I were hungry, I should not tell you,
since the world and all it holds is mine.
13 Do I eat the flesh of bulls,
or drink goats' blood?

14 "No, let thanksgiving be your sacrifice to God,
fulfil the vows you make to the Most High;
15 then you can invoke me in your troubles
and I will rescue you, and you shall honor me."

16 But to the wicked man God says:[d]

"What business have you reciting my statutes,
standing there mouthing my covenant,
17 since you detest my discipline
and thrust my words behind you?

18 "You make friends with a thief as soon as you see one,
you feel at home with adulterers,
19 your mouth is given freely to evil
and your tongue to inventing lies.

20 "You sit there, slandering your own brother,
you malign your own mother's son.
21a You do this, and expect me to say nothing?
21b Do you really think I am like you?

22 "You are leaving God out of account; take care!
Or I will tear you to pieces where no one can rescue you!
23 Whoever makes thanksgiving his sacrifice honors me;
to the upright man[e] I will show how God can save."

PSALM 51

Miserere[a]

*For the choirmaster – Psalm – Of David – When the prophet
Nathan came to him because he had been with Bathsheba*

1 Have mercy on me, O God, in your goodness,
  in your great tenderness wipe away my faults;
2 wash me clean of my guilt,
  purify me from my sin.

3 For I am well aware of my faults,
  I have my sin constantly in mind,
4 having sinned against none other than you,
  having done what you regard as wrong.

  You are just when you pass sentence on me,
  blameless when you give judgment.[b]
5 You know I was born guilty,
  a sinner from the moment of conception.[c]

6 Yet, since you love sincerity of heart,
  teach me the secrets of wisdom.[d]
7 Purify me with hyssop[e] until I am clean;
  wash me until I am whiter than snow.

8 Instill some joy and gladness into me,
  let the bones you have crushed rejoice again.
9 Hide your face from my sins,
  wipe out all my guilt.

10 God, create[f] a clean heart in me,
   put into me a new and constant spirit,
11 do not banish me from your presence,
   do not deprive me of your holy spirit.[g]

12 Be my savior again, renew my joy,
    keep my spirit steady and willing;
13 and I shall teach transgressors the way to you,
    and to you the sinners will return.

14 Save me from death,*h* God my savior,
    and my tongue will acclaim your righteousness;
15 Lord, open my lips,
    and my mouth will speak out your praise.

16 Sacrifice gives you no pleasure,
    were I to offer holocaust, you would not have it.
17 My sacrifice*i* is this broken spirit,
    you will not scorn this crushed and broken heart.

18 Show your favor graciously to Zion,
    rebuild the walls of Jerusalem.*j*
19 Then there will be proper sacrifice to please you
    —holocaust and whole oblation—*k*
    and young bulls to be offered on your altar.

PSALM 52   V 51

The fate of cynics

*For the choirmaster – Poem – Of David – When Doeg
the Edomite went and warned Saul, "David has gone
to Ahimelech's house"*

1 Why make a boast of your wickedness,
    you champion in villainy,*a*
2 all day plotting destruction?
    Your tongue is razor-sharp,
    you artist in perfidy!

3 You prefer evil to good,
    lying to honest speech;   *Pause*

88

4   you love the destructive word,
       perfidious tongue!

5   That is why God will crush you,
       snatch you away for good,
       tear you out of your tent,
    uproot you from the land of the living.   *Pause*

6   Dread will seize the virtuous at the sight,
       they will laugh at his fate:
7   "So much for the man who refused
       to make God his fortress,
    but relied on his own great wealth
       and drew his strength from crime!"

8   I, for my part, like an olive tree
       growing in the house of God,
    put my trust in God's love
       for ever and ever.

9   I mean to thank you constantly
       for doing what you did,
    and put my hope in your name, that is so full of kindness,
       in the presence of those who love you.

PSALM 53   V 52

The godless man[a]

For the choirmaster – In sickness – Poem – Of David

1   The fool says in his heart,
       "There is no God!"
    They are false, corrupt, vile,
       there is not one good man left.

2   God is looking down from heaven
        at the sons of men,
    to see if a single one is wise,
        if a single one is seeking God.

3   All have turned aside,
        all alike are tainted
    There is not one good man left,
        not a single one.

4   Are they so ignorant, these evil men
        who swallow my people
    as though they were eating bread,
        and never invoke God?

5   They will be struck with fear,
        fear without reason,
    since God scatters the bones of the apostate,[b]
        they are disgraced, for God rejects them.

6   Who will bring Israel salvation from Zion?
    When God brings his people home,
        what joy for Jacob, what happiness for Israel!

PSALM 54   V 53

An appeal to the God of justice

For the choirmaster – On stringed instruments – Poem – Of David – When the Ziphites went to Saul and said, "Is not David hiding with us?"

1   God, save me by your name,[a]
        by your power see justice done to me;
2   God, hear my prayer,
        listen to what I am saying!

3 Arrogant men[b] are attacking me,
   brutes who are hounding me to death,
   people to whom God means nothing.   *Pause*

4 But now God himself comes to help me,
   the Lord, supporter of my life.
5 May their wickedness recoil on themselves,
   Yahweh, ever faithful, destroy my enemies!

6 How gladly will I offer sacrifice to you
   and praise your name, that is so full of kindness.
7 He has rescued me from all my troubles,
   and let me see my enemies defeated.

PSALM 55   V 54

Prayer in persecution

For the choirmaster – For strings – Poem – Of David

1 God, hear my prayer,
   do not hide from my petition,
2 give me a hearing, answer me,
   I cannot rest for complaining.

3 I shudder at the enemy's shouts,
   at the howling[a] of the wicked;
   they bring misery crashing down on me,
   and vent their fury on me.

4 My heart aches in my breast,
   Death's terrors assail me,
5 fear and trembling descend on me,
   horror overwhelms me.

6 And I say,
   "Oh for the wings of a dove
   to fly away and find rest."

7   How far I would take my flight,
       and make a new home in the desert!   *Pause*

8   There I should soon find shelter
       from the raging wind,
9   and from the tempest, Lord, that destroys,
       and from their malicious tongues.[b]

I can see how Violence
       and Discord fill the city;
10   day and night they stalk together
       along the city walls.

Sorrow and Misery live inside,
11   Ruin is an inmate;
    Tyranny and Treachery are never absent
       from its central square.

12   Were it[c] an enemy who insulted me,
       I could put up with that;
    had a rival got the better of me,
       I could hide from him.

13   But you, a man of my own rank,
       a colleague and a friend,
14   to whom sweet conversation bound me
       in the house of God!

May they recoil[d] in disorder,
15   may Death descend on them,[e]
    may they go down, still living, to Sheol—
    since Evil shares their homes.

16   I, for myself, appeal to God
       and Yahweh saves me;
17   evening, morning, noon,[f]
       I complain, I groan;
    he will hear me calling.

18   His peace can ransom me
       from the war being waged on me.
    How many are ranged against me!
19   But God will hear me.

Sovereign from the first, he will humble them;   *Pause*
no change of heart for them,
    since they do not fear God.

20 He*g* has attacked his friends,
    he has gone back on his word;
21 though his mouth is smoother than butter,
    he has war in his heart;
his words may soothe more than oil,
    but they are naked swords.

22 Unload your burden on to Yahweh,
    and he will support you;
he will never permit
    the virtuous to falter.*h*

23 As for these murderous, these treacherous men,
    you, God, will push them
down to the deepest Pit
    before half their days are out.

For my part, I put my trust in you.

PSALM 56   V 55

Reliance on God

*For the choirmaster — Tune: "Dove of the distant gods"*a *—
Of David — Miktam — When the Philistines held him in Gath*

1 Take pity on me, God, as they harry me,
    pressing their attacks home all day.
2 All day my opponents harry me,
    hordes coming in to the attack.

3 Raise me up*b* when I am most afraid,
    I put my trust in you;

4 in God, whose word^c I praise,
   in God I put my trust, fearing nothing;
   what can men do to me?

5 All day long they twist what I say,
   all they think of is how to harm me,
6 they conspire, lurk, spy on my movements,
   determined to take my life.

7 Are they to go unpunished^d for such a crime?
   God, in fury bring the nations down!^e
8 You have noted my agitation,
   now collect my tears in your wineskin!^f
9 Then my enemies will have to fall back
   as soon as I call for help.

This I know: that God is on my side.
10 In God whose word I praise,
   in Yahweh, whose word I praise,
11 in God I put my trust, fearing nothing;
   what can man do to me?

12 I must fulfill the vows I made you, God;
   I shall pay you my thank offerings,
13 for you have rescued me from Death^g
   to walk in the presence of God
      in the light of the living.

PSALM 57   V 56

Among ferocious enemies

For the choirmaster – Tune: "Do not destroy" – Of David –
Miktam – When he escaped from Saul, in the cave

1 Take pity on me, God, take pity on me,
   in you my soul takes shelter;
   I take shelter in the shadow of your wings
   until the destroying storm is over.

2 I call on God the Most High,
  on God who has done everything for me:
3 to send from heaven and save me,
  to check the people harrying me,   *Pause*
  may God send his faithfulness and love.

4 I lie surrounded by lions
  greedy for human prey,
  their teeth are spears and arrows,
  their tongue a sharp sword.

5 Rise high above the heavens, God,
    let your glory be over the earth!*ᵃ*
6 They laid a net where I was walking
    when I was bowed with care;
  they dug a pitfall for me
    but fell into it themselves!   *Pause*

7 My heart is ready, God,
    my heart is ready;
  I mean to sing and play for you,
8   awake, my muse,
  awake, lyre and harp,
    I mean to wake the Dawn!*ᵇ*

9 Lord, I mean to thank you among the peoples,
    to play music to you among the nations;
10 your love is high as heaven,
    your faithfulness as the clouds.
11 Rise high above the heavens, God,
    let your glory be over the earth!

The Judge of earthly judges[a]

For the choirmaster – Tune: "Do not destroy" – Of David – Miktam

1 Gods[b] you may be, but do you give the sentences you
   should,
   and dispense impartial justice to mankind?
2 On the contrary, in your hearts you meditate oppression,
   with your hands you dole out tyranny on earth.

3 Right from the womb these wicked men have gone
   astray,
   these double talkers have been in error since their birth;
4 their poison is the poison of the snake,
   they are deaf as the adder that blocks its ears
5 so as not to hear the magician's music
   and the clever snake-charmer's spells.

6 God, break their teeth in their mouths,
   Yahweh, wrench out the fangs of these savage lions!
7 May they drain away like water running to waste,
   may they wither like trodden grass,
8 like a slug that melts as it moves,
   like an abortion,[c] denied the light of day!

9 Before they sprout thorns[d] like the bramble,
   green or scorched, may the wrath whirl them away!
10 What joy for the virtuous, seeing this vengeance,
   bathing their feet in the blood of the wicked!
11 "So," people will say, "the virtuous do have their harvest;
   so there is a God who dispenses justice on earth!"

PSALM 59

Against the wicked[a]

*For the choirmaster — Tune: "Do not destroy" — Of
David — Miktam — When Saul sent spies to his house to
have him killed*

1 Rescue me from my enemies, my God,
  protect me from those attacking me,
2 rescue me from these evil men,
  save me from these murderers!

3 Look at them lurking to ambush me,
  they are strong and united against me;
4 for no fault, no sin, no offense of mine,
  Yahweh, how they hurry into position!

  Wake up, stand by me and look,
5 Yahweh, God of Sabaoth, God of Israel,
  up, now, and punish these pagans,[b]
  show no mercy to these villains and traitors!   *Pause*

6   Back they come at nightfall,
    snarling like curs,
    prowling through the town.[c]

7 See how they slaver at the mouth,
  with swords between their teeth,
  "There is no one listening."[d]

8 Yahweh, you laugh at them,
  you make fun of these pagans.
9 My Strength, I look to you.

  My citadel is God himself,
10 the God who loves me[e] is coming,
   God will show me my enemies defeated.

97

¹¹ Slaughter them,*ʲ* God, before my people forget!
    Harry them with your power and strike them down,
      Lord, our shield!

¹² Sin is in their mouths, sin on their lips,
    so let them be caught in their pride!
    For the curses and lies they utter,

¹³ destroy them in anger, destroy, until they are finished,
    until God is acknowledged as ruler in Jacob
    to the remotest parts of the earth!   *Pause*

¹⁴   Back they come at nightfall,
      snarling like curs,
      prowling through the town;
¹⁵ scavenging for food,
    growling*ᵍ* till they are full.

¹⁶ I, for my part, celebrate your strength,
    I sing of your love morning by morning;
    you have always been my citadel,
    a shelter when I am in trouble.

¹⁷ My Strength, I play for you,
    my citadel is God himself,
      the God who loves me.

PSALM 60   V 59

National prayer after defeat*ᵃ*

*For the choirmaster – Tune: "The decree is a lily" – Miktam –
Of David – For instruction – When he was at war with Aram-
naharaim and Aram-zobah, and Joab marched back to destroy
twelve thousand Edomites in the Valley of Salt*

¹ God, you have rejected us, broken us;
    you have been angry, come back to us!

2 You have made the earth tremble, torn it apart;
  now mend the rifts, it is tottering still![b]
3 You have allowed your people to suffer,
  to drink a wine that makes us reel.

4 Hoist the standard[c] to rally those who fear you,
  to put them out of range of bow and arrow.   *Pause*
5 To bring rescue to those you love,
  save with your right hand and answer us!

6 God promised us once from his sanctuary,[d]
  "I the Victor will parcel out Shechem,
  and share out the Valley of Succoth.

7 "Gilead is mine, Manasseh mine,
  Ephraim is my helmet,
  Judah, my marshal's baton.

8 "Moab a bowl for me to wash in!
  I throw my sandal[e] over Edom.
  Now shout 'Victory,' Philistia!"[f]

9 Who is there now to take me into the fortified city,
  to lead me into Edom?
10 God, can you really have rejected us?
  You no longer march with our armies.[g]

11 Help us in this hour of crisis,
  the help that man can give is worthless.
12 With God among us we shall fight like heroes,
  he will trample on our enemies.

PSALM 61

Prayer of an exile[a]

For the choirmaster – For strings – Of David

1 God, hear my cry for help,
   listen to my prayer!
2 From the end of the earth I call to you,
   with sinking heart.

   To the rock too high for me,[b]
   lead me!
3 For you are my refuge,
   a strong tower against the enemy.

4 Let me stay in your tent for ever,
   taking refuge in the shelter of your wings.   *Pause*
5 You, God, accept my vows,
   you grant me the heritage of those who fear your name.

6 Let the king live on and on,
   prolong his years, generation on generation.
7 May he sit enthroned in God's presence for ever!
   Assign your Love and Faithfulness to guard him![c]

8 So I shall always sing of your name,
   fulfilling the vows I have taken, day after day.

Hope in God alone[a]

For the choirmaster . . . – Jeduthun – Psalm – Of David

1 In God alone there is rest for my soul,
   from him comes my safety;
2 with him alone for my rock, my safety,
   my fortress, I can never fall.
3 How many times will you come rushing at a man,
   all of you, to bring him down
   like a wall already leaning over,
   like a rampart undermined?

4 Deceit[b] their sole intention,
   their delight is to mislead;
   with lies on their lips they bless aloud,
   while cursing inwardly.   *Pause*

5 Rest in God alone, my soul!
   He is the source of my hope;
6 with him alone for my rock, my safety,
   my fortress, I can never fall;
7 rest in God, my safety, my glory,
   the rock of my strength.

8 In God, I find shelter; rely on him,
   people, at all times;
   unburden your hearts to him,
   God is a shelter for us.   *Pause*

9 Ordinary men are only a puff of wind,
   important men[c] delusion;
   put both in the scales and up they go,
   lighter than a puff of wind.

10   Put no reliance on extortion,
          no empty hopes in robbery;
       though riches may increase,
          keep your heart detached.

11   God has spoken once,
          twice I have heard this:[d]
       it is for God to be strong,
12   for you, Lord, to be loving;
       and you yourself repay
          man as his works deserve.[e]

PSALM 63

Desire for God

Psalm – Of David – When he was in the wilderness of Judah

1   God, you are my God, I am seeking you,[a]
          my soul is thirsting for you,
       my flesh is longing for you,
          a land parched, weary and waterless;
2   I long to gaze on you in the Sanctuary,
          and to see your power and glory.

3   Your love is better than life itself,
          my lips will recite your praise;
4   all my life I will bless you,
          in your name lift up my hands;
5   my soul will feast most richly,
          on my lips a song of joy and, in my mouth, praise.

6   On my bed I think of you,
          I meditate on you all night long,
7   for you have always helped me.
       I sing for joy in the shadow of your wings;
8   my soul clings close to you,
          your right hand supports me.

⁹ But may those now hounding me to death
go down to the earth below,
¹⁰ consigned to the edge of the sword,
and left as food for jackals.
¹¹ Then will the king rejoice in God,
and all who swear by him[b] be able to boast
once these lying mouths are silenced.

PSALM 64 V 63

The punishment for slanderers[a]

For the choirmaster – Psalm – Of David

¹ God, hear me as I make my plea,
protect me from this frightening enemy,
² hide me from the wicked and their schemes,
from this mob of evil men,

³ sharpening their tongues like swords,
shooting bitter words like arrows,
⁴ shooting them at the innocent from cover,
shooting suddenly, without warning.

⁵ Urging each other on to their wicked purpose,
they discuss where to hide their snares.
"Who is going to see us?" they say,
⁶ "Who can probe our secrets?"
Who? He who probes the inmost mind
and the depths of the heart.[b]

⁷ God will shoot them with his own arrow,
wound them without warning.
⁸ He will destroy them[c] for that tongue of theirs,
and all who see them fall will shake their heads.
⁹ Then all will feel afraid,
will tell others what God has done;
they will understand why he has done it.

¹⁰ The virtuous will rejoice in Yahweh,
    will make him their refuge;
and upright hearts will be able to boast.

PSALM 65 V 64
Thanksgiving hymn^a

For the choirmaster – Of David – Song

¹ Praise is rightfully yours,^b
    God, in Zion.
Vows to you must be fulfilled,
²   for you answer prayer.

All flesh must come to you
³   with all its sins;
though our faults overpower us,
    you blot them out.^c

⁴ Happy the man you choose, whom you invite
    to live in your courts.
Fill us with the good things of your house,
    of your holy Temple.

⁵ Your righteousness repays us with marvels,
    God our savior,
hope of all the ends of the earth
    and the distant islands.^d

⁶ Your strength holds the mountains up,
    such is the power that wraps you;
⁷ you calm the clamor of the ocean,
    the clamor of its waves.

⁸ The nations are in uproar,^e in panic
    those who live at the ends of the world,
as your miracles bring shouts of joy
    to the portals^f of morning and evening.

9   You visit the earth and water it,[g]
        you load it with riches;
     God's rivers brim with water[h]
        to provide their grain.

10   This is how you provide it:
     by drenching its furrows, by leveling its ridges,
     by softening it with showers, by blessing the first fruits.

11   You crown the year with your bounty,
        abundance flows wherever you pass;[i]
12   the desert pastures overflow,
        the hillsides are wrapped in joy,
13   the meadows are dressed in flocks,
        the valleys are clothed in wheat,
        what shouts of joy, what singing![j]

PSALM 66   V 65

Corporate act of thanksgiving[a]

For the choirmaster — Song — Psalm

1   Acclaim God, all the earth,
2   play music to the glory of his name,
        glorify him with your praises,
3   say to God, "What dread you inspire!"

     Your achievements are the measure of your power.
     Your enemies cringe in your presence;
4   all the earth bows down to you,
        playing music for you, playing in honor of your name.
                                                  Pause

5   Come and see what marvels God has done,
        so much to be feared for his deeds among mankind:
6   he turned the sea into dry land,
        they crossed the river on foot![b]

105

So let us rejoice in him,
7 who rules for ever by his power:
his eyes keep watch on the nations,
let no rebel raise his head!   *Pause*

8 You nations, bless our God
and make his praise resound,
9 who brings our soul to life[c]
and keeps our feet from faltering.

10 You tested us, God,
you refined us like silver,
11 you let us fall into the net,
you laid heavy burdens on our backs,
12 you let people drive over our heads;
but now the ordeal by fire and water is over,
and you allow us once more to draw breath.[d]

13 I bring holocausts to your house,
I bring them to fulfill those vows
14 that rose to my lips,
those vows I spoke when in trouble.

15 I offer you fat holocausts
and the smoke of burning rams,
I offer you bullocks and he-goats.   *Pause*

16 Come and listen, all you who fear God,
while I tell you what he has done for me:
17 when I uttered my cry to him
and high praise was on my tongue,
18 had I been guilty in my heart,
the Lord would never have heard me.
19 But God not only heard me,
he listened to my prayer.

20 Blessed be God,
who neither ignored my prayer
nor deprived me of his love.

PSALM 67

Harvest song[a]

For the choirmaster – For strings – Psalm – Song

1 May God show kindness and bless us,
and make his face smile on us!   *Pause*
2 For then the earth will acknowledge your ways
and all the nations will know of your power to save.

3 Let the nations praise you, O God,
let all the nations praise you![b]

4 Let the nations shout and sing for joy,
since you dispense true justice to the world;
you dispense strict justice[c] to the peoples,
on earth you rule the nations.   *Pause*

5 Let the nations praise you, God,
let all the nations praise you!

6 The soil has given its harvest,
God, our God, has blessed us.
7 May God bless us, and let him be feared
to the very ends of the earth.

National song of triumph[a]

For the choirmaster – Of David – Psalm – Song

1 Let God arise, let his enemies be scattered,
   let those who hate him flee before him!
2 As smoke disperses, they disperse;[b]
   as wax melts when near the fire,
   so the wicked perish when God approaches.

3 But at God's approach, the virtuous rejoice,
   exulting and singing for joy.
4 Sing to Yahweh, play music to his name,
   build a road for the Rider of the Clouds,
   rejoice[c] in Yahweh, exult at his coming!

5 Father of orphans, defender of widows,
   such is God in his holy dwelling;
6 God gives the lonely a permanent home,
   makes prisoners happy by setting them free,
   but rebels must live in an arid land.

7 God, when you set out at the head of your people,
8 and marched across the desert, the earth rocked,
                                        Pause

   the heavens deluged at God's coming,[d]
   at the coming of God, the God of Israel.

9 God, you rained a downpour of blessings,
   when your heritage was faint you gave it strength;
10 your family found a home, where you
   in your goodness, God, provided for the needy.[e]

11a The Lord gives his couriers the news,
14a "Shaddai has scattered a huge army."*f*
11b
12 Kings are in flight, armies in flight,
the women at home take their pick of the loot.*g*

13 Meanwhile you others were lolling in the sheepfolds.*h*
There were dove wings covered with silver,
on their pinions the sheen of green gold;
14b jewels were there like snow on Dark Mountain.*i*

15 That peak of Bashan, a mountain of God?
Rather, a mountain of pride, that peak of Bashan!
16 Peaks of pride, have you the right to look down on
a mountain where God has chosen to live,*j*
where Yahweh is going to live for ever?

17 With thousands of myriads of divine chariots*k*
the Lord has left Sinai for his sanctuary.*l*
18 God, you have ascended to the height,*m* and captured
prisoners,
you have taken men as tribute,
yes, taken rebels to your dwelling, Yahweh!*n*

19 Blessed be the Lord day after day,
the God who saves us and bears our burdens!

20 This God of ours is a God who saves,
to the Lord Yahweh belong the ways of escape from
death;
21 but God will smash the heads of his enemies,
the hairy skull of the man who parades his guilt.

22 The Lord has promised, "I will bring them back from
Bashan,
I will bring them back from the bottom of the sea,
23 for your feet to wade in blood,
for the tongues of your dogs to lap their share of the
enemy."*o*

24 God, your procession can be seen,
   my God's, my king's procession to the sanctuary,
25 with cantors marching in front, musicians behind,
   and between them maidens playing tambourines.

26   Bless God in your choirs,
     bless the Lord, you who spring from Israel![p]

27 Benjamin, the youngest, is there in the lead,[q]
   the princes of Judah in brocaded robes,
   the princes of Zebulun, the princes of Naphtali.[r]

28 Take command, God, as befits your power,[s]
   that power, God, you have wielded on our behalf
29 from your Temple high above Jerusalem!
   Kings will come to you, bringing presents.

30 Rebuke the Beast of the Reeds,[t]
   that herd of bulls, those calves, that people,
   until, humbled, they bring gold and silver.
   Scatter those warmongering pagans!

31 Ambassadors[u] will come from Egypt,
   Ethiopia will stretch out her hands to God.

32 Sing to God, you kingdoms of the earth,
33 play for[v] the Rider of the Heavens, the ancient heavens!
                                                    Pause

   Listen to him shouting, to his thundering,
34 and acknowledge the power of God!

   Over Israel his splendor, in the clouds his power,
35 God in his[w] sanctuary is greatly to be feared.
   He, the God of Israel,
   gives power and strength to his people.

   Blessed be God.

Lament[a]

For the choirmaster – Tune: "Lilies . . ." – Of David

1 Save me, God! The water
  is already up to my neck![b]

2 I am sinking in the deepest swamp,
  there is no foothold;
I have stepped into deep water
  and the waves are washing over me.

3 Worn out with calling, my throat is hoarse,
my eyes are strained, looking for my God.

4 More people hate me for no reason
  than I have hairs on my head,
more are groundlessly hostile
  than I have hair to show.[c]
(They ask me to give back what I never took.)[d]

5 God, you know how foolish I have been,
my offenses are not hidden from you;

6 but let those who hope in you not blush for me,
  Yahweh Sabaoth![e]
Let those who seek you not be ashamed of me,
  God of Israel!

7 It is for you I am putting up with insults
that cover me with shame,

8 that make me a stranger to my brothers,
an alien to my mother's other sons;

9 zeal for your house devours me,
and the insults of those who insult you fall on me.

10 If I mortify[j] myself with fasting,
   they make this a pretext for insulting me;
11 if I dress myself in sackcloth,
   I become their laughingstock,
12 the gossip of people sitting at the city gate,
   and the theme of drunken songs.

13 For my part, I pray to you, Yahweh,
      at the time you wish;
   in your great love, answer me, God,
      faithful in saving power.

14 Pull me out of this swamp; let me sink no farther,
      let me escape those who hate me,
      save me from deep water!
15 Do not let the waves wash over me,
      do not let the deep swallow me
   or the Pit close its mouth on me.

16 In your loving kindness, answer me; Yahweh,
   in your great tenderness turn to me;
17 do not hide your face from your servant,
   quick, I am in trouble, answer me;
18 come to my side, redeem me,
   from so many enemies ransom me.

19a You know all the insults I endure,
19c every one of my oppressors is known to you;
20a the insults have broken my heart,
19b
20b my shame and disgrace are past cure;[g]
   I had hoped for sympathy, but in vain,
20c I found no one to console me.

21 They gave me poison to eat instead,
   when I was thirsty they gave me vinegar to drink.

22 May their own table prove a trap for them,
   and their plentiful supplies, a snare!
23 may their eyes grow dim, go blind,
   strike their loins with chronic palsy!

24 Vent your fury on them,
let your burning anger overtake them;
25 may their camp be reduced to ruin,
and their tents left unoccupied:
26 for hounding a man after you had struck him,
for adding more wounds to those which you inflicted.[h]

27 Charge them with crime after crime,
deny them further access to your righteousness,
28 blot them out of the book of life,
strike them off the roll of the virtuous!

29 For myself, wounded wretch that I am,
by your saving power, God, lift me up!
30 I will praise the name of God with a song,
I will extol him with my thanksgiving,
31 more pleasing to Yahweh than any ox
or bull with horn and hoof.

32 Then, seeing this, the humble can rejoice:
long life to your hearts, all you who seek for God!
33 Yahweh will always hear those who are in need,
will never scorn his captive people.
34 Let heaven and earth acclaim him,
the oceans and all that moves in them!

35 For God will save Zion,
and rebuild the towns of Judah:
they will be lived in, owned,
36 handed down to his servants' descendants,
and lived in by those who love his name.

PSALM 70

A cry of distress[a]

For the choirmaster – Of David – For commemoration

1 Oh come and rescue me, God,
   Yahweh come quickly and help me!
2 Shame and dishonor on those
   who are out to kill me!

   Down with them! Disgrace on those
   who enjoy my misfortune!
3 May they be aghast with shame,
   those who say to me, "Aha! Aha!"

4 But joy and gladness
   for all who seek you!
   To all who love your saving power
   give constant cause to say, "God is great!"

5 To me, poor wretch,
   come quickly, God!
   My helper, my savior, Yahweh,
   come without delay!

PSALM 71

An old man's prayer

1 In you, Yahweh, I take shelter;
   never let me be disgraced.
2 In your righteousness rescue me, deliver me,
   turn your ear to me and save me!

3   Be a sheltering rock for me,
    a walled fortress[a] to save me!
    For you are my rock, my fortress.
4   My God, rescue me from the hands of the wicked,
    from the clutches of rogue and tyrant!

5   For you alone are my hope, Lord,
    Yahweh, I have trusted you since my youth,
6   I have relied on you since I was born,
    you have been my portion[b] from my mother's womb,
    and the constant theme of my praise.

7   To many I have seemed an enigma,[c]
    but you are my firm refuge.
8   My mouth is full of your praises,
    filled with your splendor all day long.

9   Do not reject me now I am old,
    nor desert me now my strength is failing,
10 for my enemies are uttering threats,
    spies hatching their conspiracy:

11 "Hound him down now that God has deserted him,
    seize him, there is no one to rescue him!"
12 God, do not stand aside,
    my God, come quickly and help me!

13 Shame and ruin on those
        who attack me;
    may insult and disgrace cover those
        whose aim is to hurt me!

14 I promise that, ever hopeful,
        I will praise you more and more,
15 my lips shall proclaim your righteousness
        and power to save, all day long.[d]

16 I will come[e] in the power of Yahweh
    to commemorate your righteousness, yours alone.
17 God, you taught me when I was young,
    and I am still proclaiming your marvels.

18 Now that I am old and gray,
 God, do not desert me;^f
 let me live to tell the rising generation
 about your strength^g and power,
19 about your heavenly righteousness, God.

 You have done great things;
 who, God, is comparable to you?
20 You have sent me misery and hardship,
 but you will give me life again,
 you will pull me up again from the depths of the earth,
21 prolong my old age, and once more comfort me.

22 I promise I will thank you on the lyre,
  my ever-faithful God,
 I will play the harp in your honor,
  Holy One of Israel.

23 My lips shall sing for joy as I play to you,
  and this soul of mine which you have redeemed.
24 And all day long, my tongue
  shall be talking of your righteousness.
 Shame and disgrace on those
  whose aim is to hurt me!

PSALM 72   V 71

The promised king^a

Of Solomon

1 God, give your own justice to the king,
  your own righteousness to the royal son,
2 so that he may rule your people rightly
  and your poor with justice.

³ Let the mountains and hills
  bring a message of peace for the people.
⁴ Uprightly[b] he will defend the poorest,
  he will save the children of those in need,
  and crush their oppressors.

⁵ Like sun and moon he will endure,[c]
  age after age,
⁶ welcome as rain that falls on the pasture,[d]
  and showers to thirsty soil.

⁷ In his days virtue[e] will flourish,
  a universal peace till the moon is no more;[f]
⁸ his empire shall stretch from sea to sea,
  from the river to the ends of the earth.[g]

⁹ The Beast[h] will cower before him
  and his enemies grovel in the dust;
¹⁰ the kings of Tarshish and of the islands
  will pay him tribute.

  The kings of Sheba and Seba
  will offer gifts;
¹¹ all kings will do him homage,
  all nations become his servants.

¹² He will free the poor man who calls to him,
  and those who need help,
¹³ he will have pity on the poor and feeble,
  and save the lives of those in need;

¹⁴ he will redeem their lives from exploitation and outrage,
  their lives will be precious in his sight.
¹⁵ (Long may he live, may gold from Sheba be given him!)[i]
  Prayer will be offered for him constantly,
  blessings invoked on him all day long.[j]

¹⁶ Grain everywhere in the country,
  even on the mountain tops,
  abundant as Lebanon its harvest,
  luxuriant as common grass![k]

¹⁷ Blessed be his name for ever,
enduring as long as the sun!^l
May every race in the world be blessed in him,
and all the nations call him blessed!

¹⁸ Blessed be Yahweh, the God of Israel,
who alone performs these marvels!
¹⁹ Blessed for ever be his glorious name,
may the whole world be filled with his glory!
Amen. Amen!

²⁰ End of the prayers of David, son of Jesse.^m

PSALM 73   V 72

The triumph of justice^a

Psalm – Of Asaph

¹ God is indeed good to Israel,^b
the Lord is good to pure hearts.^c

² My feet were on the point of stumbling,
a little farther and I should have slipped,
³ envying the arrogant as I did,
and watching the wicked get rich.

⁴ For them,^d no such thing as pain,
their bodies are healthy and strong,
⁵ they do not suffer as other men do,
no human afflictions for them!

⁶ So pride is their chain of honor,
violence the garment that covers them;
⁷ their spite oozes like fat,^e
their hearts drip with slyness.

8 Cynical advocates of evil,
   lofty advocates of force,
9 they think their mouth is heaven
   and their tongue can dictate on earth.[f]

10 This is why my people turn to them
   and lap up all they say,[g]
11 asking, "How will God find out?
   Does the Most High know everything?
12 Look at them: these are the wicked,
   well-off and still getting richer!"

13 After all, why should I keep my own heart pure,
   and wash my hands in innocence,
14 if you plague me all day long
   and discipline me every morning?

15 Had I said, "That talk appeals to me,"
   I should have betrayed your children's race.
16 Instead, I tried to analyze the problem,
   hard though I found it—

17 until the day I pierced the mystery[h]
   and saw the end in store for them:
18 they are on a slippery slope, you put them there,
   you urge them on to ruin,

19 until suddenly they fall,
   done for, terrified to death.
20 When you wake up, Lord, you shrug them off
   like the phantoms of a morning dream.[i]

21 When my heart had been growing sourer
   with pains shooting through my loins,
22 I had simply failed to understand,
   my stupid attitude to you was brutish.[j]

23 Even so, I stayed in your presence,
   you held my right hand;
24 now guide me with advice
   and in the end receive me into glory.[k]

25 I look to no one else in heaven,
   I delight in nothing else on earth.
26 My flesh and my heart are pining with love,[l]
   my heart's Rock, my own, God for ever!

27 So then: those who abandon you are doomed,
   you destroy the adulterous deserter;[m]
28 whereas my joy lies in being close to God.
   I have taken shelter in the Lord,
   continually to proclaim what you have done.[n]

PSALM 74   V 73

Lament on the destruction of the Temple[a]

Poem – Of Asaph

1 God, have you finally rejected us,
   raging at the flock you used to pasture?
2 Remember the people you long since made your own,
   your hereditary tribe whom you redeemed,
   and this Mount Zion where you came to live.

3 Pick your steps over these endless ruins:
   the enemy have sacked everything in the sanctuary.
4 They roared where your Assemblies used to take place,
   they stuck their enemy emblems over the entrance,[b]
5 emblems we had never seen before.[c]

6 Axes deep in the wood, hacking at the panels,
   they battered them down with mallet and hatchet;
7 then, God, setting fire to your sanctuary,
   they profanely razed the house of your name to the
   ground.

8 Determined to destroy us*d* once and for all,
  they burned down every shrine of God in the country.
9 Deprived of signs, with no prophets left,
  who can say how long this will last?*e*

10 How much longer, God, is the oppressor to blaspheme,
   is the enemy to insult your name for ever?
11 Why hold back your hand,
   why keep your right hand hidden?*f*

12 Yet, God, my king from the first,
   author of saving acts throughout the earth,
13 by your power you split the sea in two,
   and smashed the heads of monsters on the waters.

14 You crushed Leviathan's heads,*g*
   leaving him for wild animals*h* to eat,
15 you opened the spring, the torrent,
   you dried up inexhaustible rivers.*i*

16 You are master of day and night,
   you instituted light and sun,
17 you fixed the boundaries of the world,
   you created summer and winter.

18 Now, Yahweh, remember the enemy's blasphemy,
   how frenzied people dare to insult your name.
19 Do not betray your turtledove to the beast,*j*
   do not forget your wretched people for good.

20 Respect the covenant! We can bear no more—
   every cave in the country is the scene of violence!
21 Do not let the hard-pressed retreat in confusion,
   give the poor and needy cause to praise your name.

22 Rise, God, say something on your own behalf,
   do not forget the madman's daylong blaspheming,
23 remember the shouting of your enemies,
   this ever-rising clamor of your adversaries.

To the divine judge[a]

For the choirmaster – Tune: "Do not destroy" – Psalm –
Of Asaph – Song

1　We give thanks to you, God,
　　we give thanks as we invoke your name,
　　as we recount your marvels.[b]

2　"at the moment I decide
　　I will dispense strict justice;
3　the earth shall quake and all its inhabitants,
　　it is I who poised its columns.

4　"I said to the boastful: Enough of boasting!
　　and to the wicked: How dare you raise your horn,[c]
5　how dare you raise your horn like that,
　　how dare you speak so boldly!"

6　Not from the east, nor from the west,
　　not from the desert, nor from the mountains,[d]
7　but from God the judgment comes,
　　lowering one, raising another.

8　Yahweh is holding a cup
　　of frothing wine, heavily drugged;[e]
　　he pours it out, they drain it to the dregs,[f]
　　all drink of it, the wicked of the earth.

9　But I will never stop proclaiming the God of Jacob
　　or playing in his honor;
10　I will cut off the horns of all the wicked
　　and raise the horns of the virtuous.

Ode to God the awe-inspiring[a]

For the choirmaster – For strings – Psalm – Of Asaph

1 God is renowned in Judah,
  his name is great in Israel;
2 his tent is pitched in Salem,[b]
  his home is in Zion;
3 there he has broken the lightning-swift arrow,[c]
  the shield, the sword and the line of battle.[d]   *Pause*

4 You the Illustrious and Majestic:
5 mountains of spoil have been captured;[e]
  heroes are now sleeping their last sleep,
  the warriors' arms have failed them;
6 at your reproof, God of Jacob,
  chariot and horse stand spellbound.

7 You the Terrible! Who can oppose you
  and your furious onslaught?[f]
8 When your verdicts thunder from heaven,
  earth stays silent with dread;
9 when God stands up to give judgment
  and to save all the humble of the earth.   *Pause*

10 Man's wrath only adds to your glory;[g]
  the survivors of your wrath you will draw like a girdle
    around you;[h]
11 fulfill the promises you make to Yahweh your God,
  make offerings to the Terrible, you who surround him;[i]
12 he snuffs out the lives of princes,
  he is terrible to the kings of the earth.

Meditation on Israel's past[a]

For the choirmaster . . . – Jeduthum – Of Asaph – Psalm

1 Loudly I cry to God,
  loudly to God who hears me.

2 When in trouble I sought the Lord,
  all night long I stretched out my hands,
  my soul refusing to be consoled.

3 I thought of God and sighed,
  I pondered and my spirit failed me.

4 You stopped me closing my eyes,
  I was too distraught to speak;

5 I thought of the olden days,

6 years long past came back to me,
  I spent all night meditating[b] in my heart,
  I pondered and my spirit asked this question:

7 "If the Lord has rejected you, is this final?
  If he withholds his favor, is this for ever?

8 Is his love over for good
  and the promise void for all time?

9 Has God forgotten to show mercy,
  or has his anger overcome his tenderness?   *Pause*

10 "This," I said then, "is what distresses me:[c]
   that the power in the Most High is no longer what it
      was."

11 Remembering[d] Yahweh's achievements,
   remembering your marvels in the past,

12 I reflect on all that you did,
   I ponder on all your achievements.

13 God, your ways are holy!
  What god so great as God?
14 You are the God who did marvelous things
  and forced nations to acknowledge your power,
15 with your own arm redeeming your people,
  the sons of Jacob and Joseph.   *Pause*

16 When the waters saw it was you, God,
  when the waters saw it was you, they recoiled,
  shuddering to their depths.
17 The clouds poured down water,
  the sky thundered,
  your arrows darted out.[e]

18 Your thunder crashed as it rolled,
  your lightning lit up the world,
  the earth shuddered and quaked.
19 You strode across the sea,
  you marched across the ocean,
  but your steps could not be seen.

20 You guided your people like a flock
  by the hands of Moses and Aaron.

PSALM 78   V 77

The lessons of Israelite history[a]

Psalm – Of Asaph

1 Listen to this Law, my people,
  pay attention to what I say;
2 I am going to speak to you in parable[b]
  and expound the mysteries of our past.

³ What we have heard and known for ourselves,
and what our ancestors have told us,
⁴ must not be withheld from their descendants,
but be handed on by us to the next generation;

this is: the titles of Yahweh, his power
and the miracles he has done.
⁵ When he issued the decrees for Jacob
and instituted a Law in Israel,

he gave our ancestors strict orders
to teach it to their children;
⁶ the next generation was to learn it,
the children still to be born,

and these in their turn were to tell their own children
⁷ so that they too would put their confidence in God,
never forgetting God's achievements,
and always keeping his commandments,

⁸ and not becoming, like their ancestors,
a stubborn and unruly generation,
a generation with no sincerity of heart,
in spirit unfaithful to God.

⁹ The sons of Ephraim, who were bowmen,
turned tail when the time came to fight;[c]
¹⁰ they had not kept God's covenant,
they refused to follow his Law;

¹¹ they had forgotten his achievements,
the marvels he had shown them:[d]
¹² he had worked wonders for their ancestors
in the plains of Zoan, down in Egypt:

¹³ dividing the sea, bringing them through,
making the waters stand up like dikes,
¹⁴ leading them with a cloud by day
and with a fiery glow at night,

15 splitting rocks in the wilderness,
   quenching their thirst with unlimited water,
16 conjuring streams from the rock
   and bringing down water in torrents.

17 They only sinned against him more than ever,
   defying the Most High in the desert,
18 deliberately challenging God
   by demanding their favorite food.

19 They blasphemed against God,
   "Is it likely," they said, "that God
   could give a banquet in the wilderness?

20 "Admittedly, when he struck the rock,
   waters gushed, torrents streamed out,
   but bread now, can he give us that,
   can he provide meat for his people?"

21 Yahweh was enraged when he heard them,
   a fire flared at Jacob,
   the wrath attacked Israel
22 for having no faith in God,
   no trust in his power to save.

23 He gave orders to the skies above,
   he opened the doors of heaven,
24 he rained down manna to feed them,
   he gave them the wheat of heaven;
25 men ate the bread of Immortals,[e]
   he sent them more food than they could eat.

26 He stirred up an east wind in the heavens,
   he conjured up a south wind by his power,
27 he rained down meat on them like dust;
   birds as thick as sand on the seashore
28 he sent tumbling into their camp,
   in all directions round their tents.

29 They all had enough and to spare,
   he having provided what they wanted;

30 but they had hardly satisfied their craving,
the food was still in their mouths,

31 when the wrath of God attacked them,
slaughtering their strongest men
and laying the flower of Israel low.

32 Despite all this they went on sinning,*f*
and put no faith in his marvels;
33 for which he blasted their days
and their years in a flash.*g*

34 Whenever he slaughtered them they sought him,
they came to their senses and sought him earnestly
35 remembering that God was their rock,
God the Most High, their redeemer.

36 But though they outwardly flattered him
and used their tongues to lie to him,
37 in their hearts they were not true to him,
they were unfaithful to his covenant.

38 Compassionately, however,
he forgave their guilt instead of killing them,
repeatedly repressing his anger
instead of rousing his full wrath,
39 remembering they were creatures of flesh,
a puff of wind that passes and does not return.

40 How often they defied him in the wilderness,
how often they outraged him in the desert,
41 repeatedly challenging God,
provoking the Holy One of Israel—
42 entirely oblivious of his hand
and of the time he saved them from the oppressor:

43 by imposing his signs*h* on Egypt,
by displaying his wonders in the plains of Zoan,
44 by turning their rivers into blood
to stop them drinking from their streams,

45 by sending horseflies to eat them
and frogs to devastate them,
46 by consigning their crops to the caterpillar
and their hard-won harvest to the locust,

47 by killing their vines with hail
and their sycamore trees with frost,
48 by condemning their cattle to plague[i]
and their flocks to feverish pests,

49 by unleashing his fierce anger, rage,
indignation and hardship on them,
a mission of angels of disaster,
50 by giving his anger free rein,

by not even exempting them from death,
by condemning them to plague,
51 by striking down all the firstborn in Egypt,
the first fruits of their virility in the tents of Ham,

52 by driving his people out like sheep,[j]
by leading them through the wilderness like a flock,
53 by guiding them safe and unafraid
while the sea engulfed their enemies,

54 by bringing them to his sacred frontier,
the highlands conquered by his own right hand,
55 by expelling the pagans in front of them
and by marking out a heritage for each,
in which the tribes of Israel could pitch their tents.

56 Even so, they went on challenging God the Most High,
rebelliously disregarding his decrees;[k]
57 as perverse and disloyal as their ancestors,
treacherous as a bow with a warp,
58 provoking him with their high places
and rousing his jealousy with their idols.

59 God was enraged when he heard them,
he rejected Israel out of hand,
60 he left his home in Shiloh,
that tent where he once lived with men.

61 He consigned his power to captivity,
his splendor[l] to the enemy's clutches;
62 he condemned his own people to the sword,
he raged at his heritage,

63 whose young men were then burnt to death—
no brides left to hear the wedding song;
64 whose priests fell by the sword—
no widows left to raise the dirge.

65 Then, like a sleeper, like a hero
fighting-mad with wine, the Lord woke up
66 to strike his enemies on the rump[m]
and put them to everlasting shame.

67 Rejecting the tent of Joseph,[n]
not choosing the tribe of Ephraim,
68 instead he chose the tribe of Judah
and his well-loved mountain of Zion,
69 where he built his sanctuary, a copy of high heaven,[o]
founding it firm as the earth for ever.

70 Choosing David as his servant,
he took him from the sheepfolds,
71 called him from tending ewes in lamb
to pasture his people Jacob
and Israel his heritage:
72 who did this with unselfish care
and led them with a sensitive hand.

PSALM 79

National lament[a]

Psalm – Of Asaph

1 God, the pagans have invaded your heritage,
they have desecrated your holy Temple;
they have reduced Jerusalem to a pile of ruins,

2 they have left the corpses of your servants
to the birds of the air for food,
and the flesh of your devout to the beasts of the earth.

3 They have shed blood like water
throughout Jerusalem, not a gravedigger left!

4 we are now insulted by our neighbors,
butt and laughingstock of all those around us.

5 How much longer will you be angry, Yahweh? For ever?
Is your jealousy to go on smoldering like a fire?

6 Pour out your anger on the pagans,
who do not acknowledge you,
and on those kingdoms
that do not call on your name,

7 for they have devoured Jacob
and reduced his home to desolation.

8 Do not hold our ancestors' crimes against us,
in tenderness quickly intervene,
we can hardly be crushed lower;

9 help us, God our savior,
for the honor of your name;
Yahweh, blot out our sins,
rescue us for the sake of your name.

10 Why should the pagans ask, "Where is their God?"
   May we soon see the pagans learning what vengeance
   you exact for your servants'[b] blood shed here!
11 May the groans of the captive reach you;
   by your mighty arm rescue those doomed to die!

12 Pay our neighbors sevenfold, strike to the heart
   for the monstrous insult proffered to you, Lord!
13 And we your people, the flock that you pasture,
       giving you everlasting thanks,
       will recite your praises for ever and ever.

PSALM 80   V 79

Prayer for the restoration of Israel[a]

For the choirmaster – Tune: "The decrees are lilies" –
Of Asaph – Psalm

1 Shepherd of Israel, listen,
   you who lead Joseph like a flock;
   enthroned on the cherubs, shine
2 on Ephraim, Benjamin, and Manasseh;[b]
   rouse your strength,
   come to us and save us!

3 Yahweh Sabaoth,[c] bring us back,
   let your face smile on us and we shall be safe.

4 Yahweh[d] Sabaoth, how much longer
   will you smolder at your people's prayer?
5 Having fed us on the bread of tears,
   having made us drink them in such measure,
6 you now let our neighbors quarrel over us
   and our enemies deride us.

7 Yahweh Sabaoth, bring us back,
    let your face smile on us and we shall be safe.

8 There was a vine:*e* you uprooted it from Egypt;
    to plant it, you drove out other nations,
9 you cleared a space where it could grow,
    it took root and filled the whole country.

10 It covered the mountains with its shade,
    the cedars of God*f* with its branches,
11 its tendrils extended to the sea,
    its offshoots all the way to the river.*g*

12 Why have you destroyed its fences?
    Now anyone can go and steal its grapes,
13 the forest boar can ravage it
    and wild animals eat it.

14 Please, Yahweh Sabaoth, relent!
    Look down from heaven, look at this vine,
15 visit it, protect
    what your own right hand has planted.*h*
16 They threw it on the fire like dung,*i*
    but one look of reproof from you
    and they will be doomed.

17 May your hand protect the man at your right,
    the son of man who has been authorized by you.*j*
18 We shall never turn from you again;
    our life renewed, we shall invoke your name.

19 Yahweh Sabaoth, bring us back,
    let your face smile on us and we shall be safe.

For the feast of Tabernacles[a]

For the choirmaster – On the . . . of Gath – Of Asaph

1 Shout for joy to honor God our strength,
   shout to acclaim the God of Jacob!

2 Start the music, sound the drum,
   the melodious lyre and the harp;
3 sound the New Moon trumpet,
   at the full moon, on our feastday![b]

4 This is a statute binding on Israel,
   an ordinance of the God of Jacob,
5 this decree he imposed on Joseph
   when he went to war against[c] Egypt.

   I can hear[d] a voice I no longer recognize,
6 "It was I who relieved your shoulder of the burden,
   your hands could drop the laborer's basket;[e]
7 you called in your trouble, so I rescued you.

   "Hidden in the storm, I answered you,[f]
   I tested you at the waters of Meribah.   *Pause*
8 Listen, you are my people, let me warn you.
   Israel, if you would only listen to me!

9 "Tolerate no foreign god,
   worship no alien god;
10 I, Yahweh, am your God,
   I who brought you here from Egypt;
   you have only to open your mouth for me to fill it.

11 "My people refused to listen to me,
   Israel refused to obey me,
12 so I left them to their stubborn selves
   to do whatever they pleased.

13 "If only my people would listen,
   if Israel would follow my ways,
14 at one blow I would defeat their enemies
   and strike at all who attack them.

15 "Then those who hate Yahweh would cringe,
   their doom being sealed for ever;
16 while I would feed you on pure wheat
   and satisfy you with the wild rock honey."

PSALM 82   V 81

Against corrupt judges[a]

Psalm – Of Asaph

1 God stands in the divine assembly,
   among the gods he dispenses justice:

2 "No more mockery of justice,[b]
   no more favoring the wicked!   *Pause*
3 Let the weak and the orphan have justice,
   be fair to the wretched and destitute;
4 rescue the weak and needy,
   save them from the clutches of the wicked!"

5 Ignorant and senseless, they carry on blindly,
   undermining the very basis of earthly society.
6 I once said, "You too are gods,
   sons of the Most High, all of you,"[c]
7 but all the same, you shall die like other men;
   as one man, princes, you shall fall.

135

⁸ Rise, God, dispense justice throughout the world,
since no nation is excluded from your ownership.

PSALM 83 V 82

Against the enemies of Israel^a

Song — Psalm — Of Asaph

¹ God, do not remain silent;
do not be unmoved, O God, or unresponsive!
² See how your enemies are stirring,
see how those who hate you rear their heads.

³ Weaving a plot against your people,
⁴ conspiring against those you protect, they say,
"Come, we will finish them as a nation,
the name of Israel shall be forgotten!"

⁵ Unanimous^b in their plot,
they seal a treaty against you:
⁶ the tents of Edom and the Ishmaelites,
Moab and the Hagarites,^c

⁷ Gebal,^d Ammon, Amalek,
Philistia and the Tyrians;
⁸ and now Assur^e has joined them
to reinforce the sons of Lot.   *Pause*

⁹ Treat them like Midian and Sisera,
like Jabin at the river Kishon,
¹⁰ wiped out at En-dor,
they served to dung the ground.

¹¹ Treat their generals like Oreb and Zeeb,
their commanders like Zebah and Zalmunna,
¹² those who once said, "Let us take for ourselves
possession of the Dwellings of God!"

13 My God, bowl them along like tumbleweed,^f
   like chaff at the mercy of the wind;
14 as fire devours the forest,
   as the flame licks up the mountains,

15 drive them on with your whirlwind,
   rout them with your tornado;
16 cover their faces with shame,
   until they seek your name, Yahweh.

17 Shame and panic be always theirs,
18 disgrace and death; and let them know this:
   you alone bear the name Yahweh,
   Most High over the whole world.

PSALM 84 V 83

Pilgrimage song^a

*For the choirmaster – On the . . . of Gath – Of the sons of
Korah – Psalm*

1 How I love your palace,
     Yahweh Sabaoth!
2 How my soul yearns and pines
     for Yahweh's courts!
   My heart and my flesh sing for joy
     to the living God.

3 The sparrow has found its home at last,
   the swallow a nest for its young,
   your altars, Yahweh Sabaoth,
     my king and my God.

4 Happy those who live in your house
     and can praise you all day long;   *Pause*

⁵ and happy the pilgrims inspired by you
  with courage to make the Ascents!ᵇ

⁶ As they go through the Valley of the Weeper,ᶜ
  they make it a place of springs,
  clothed in blessingsᵈ by early rains.

⁷ Thence they make their way from height to height,
  soon to be seen before God on Zion.ᵉ

⁸ Yahwehᶠ Sabaoth, hear my prayer,
  listen, God of Jacob;   *Pause*

⁹ God our shield, now look on us
  and be kind to your anointed.ᵍ

¹⁰ A single day in your courts
   is worth more than a thousand elsewhere;
   merely to stand on the steps of God'sʰ house
   is better than living with the wicked.

¹¹ For God is battlementⁱ and shield,
   conferring grace and glory;
   Yahweh withholds nothing good
   from those who walk without blame.

¹² Yahweh Sabaoth,
   happy the man who puts his trust in you!

PSALM 85   V 84

Prayer for peaceᵃ

For the choirmaster – Of the sons of Korah – Psalm

¹ Yahweh, you favor your own country,
  you bring back the captives of Jacob,

² you take your people's guilt away,
  you blot out all their sins,   *Pause*

3 you retract all your anger,
    you abjure your fiery rage.

4 Bring us back, God our savior,
    master your resentment against us.
5 Do you mean to be angry with us for ever,
    to prolong your wrath age after age?

6 Will you not give us life again,
    for your people to rejoice in you?
7 Yahweh, show us your love,
    grant us your saving help.

8 I am listening. What is Yahweh saying?
    What God is saying means peace
    for his people, for his friends,
    if only they renounce their folly;
9 for those who fear him, his saving help is near,
    and the glory will then live in our country.[b]

10 Love and Loyalty now meet,
    Righteousness and Peace now embrace;[c]
11 Loyalty reaches up from earth
    and Righteousness leans down from heaven.

12 Yahweh himself bestows happiness
    as our soil gives its harvest,
13 Righteousness always preceding him
    and Peace[d] following his footsteps.

PSALM 86

Prayer in ordeal

Prayer – Of David

1 Listen to me, Yahweh, and answer me,
poor and needy as I am;
2 keep my soul: I am your devoted one,
save your servant who relies on you.

3 You are my God, take pity on me, Lord,
I invoke you all day long;
4 give your servant reason to rejoice,
for to you, Lord, I lift my soul.

5 Lord, you are good and forgiving,
most loving to all who invoke you;
6 Yahweh, hear my prayer,
listen to me as I plead.

7 Lord, in trouble I invoke you,
and you answer my prayer;
8 there is no god to compare with you,
no achievement to compare with yours.[a]

9 All the pagans[b] will come and adore you, Lord,
all will glorify your name,
10 since you alone are great, you perform marvels,
you God, you alone.

11 Yahweh, teach me your way,
how to walk beside you faithfully,
make me singlehearted in fearing your name.

12 I thank you with all my heart, Lord my God,
I glorify your name for ever,

13 your love for me has been so great,
   you have rescued me from the depths of Sheol.

14 Now arrogant men, God, are attacking me,
   a brutal gang hounding me to death:
   people to whom you mean nothing.

15 Lord God, you who are always merciful and tender-
      hearted,
   slow to anger, always loving, always loyal,
16 turn to me and pity me.

   Give me your strength, your saving help,
   me your servant, this son of a pious mother,
17 give me one proof of your goodness.

   Yahweh, make my opponents ashamed,
   show them that you are my help and consolation.

PSALM 87   V 86

Zion, mother of nations[a]

Of the sons of Korah – Psalm – Song

2a
1   Yahweh loves his city
        founded on the holy mountain;
2b   he prefers the gates of Zion
2c   to any town in Jacob.
 3   He has glorious predictions to make[b] of you,
        city of God!   *Pause*

 4   "I will add Egypt and Babylon
        to the nations that acknowledge me.
     Of Philistia, Tyre, Ethiopia,
        'Here so and so was born,' men say.
 5   But all call Zion 'Mother,'[c]
        since all were born in her."[d]

141

It is he who makes her what she is,
6   he, the Most High, Yahweh;
and as he registers the peoples,[e]
    "It was here" he writes "that so and so was born."
                                                    Pause

7   And there will be princes dancing there.[f]
    All find their home in you.[g]

PSALM 88

Lament[a]

*Song – Psalm – Of the sons of Korah – For the choirmaster –
In sickness or suffering – Poem – For Heman the native-born*

1   Yahweh my God, I call for help all day,[b]
    I weep to you all night;
2   may my prayer reach you
    hear my cries for help;

3   for my soul is all troubled,
    my life is on the brink of Sheol;
4   I am numbered among those who go down to the Pit,
    a man bereft of strength:

5   a man alone,[c] down among the dead,
    among the slaughtered in their graves,
    among those you have forgotten,
    those deprived of your protecting hand.

6   You have plunged me to the bottom of the Pit,
    to its darkest, deepest place,
7   weighted down by your anger,
    drowned beneath your waves.   *Pause*

8   You have turned my friends against me
    and made me repulsive to them;
    in prison and unable to escape,
9   my eyes are worn out with suffering.

    Yahweh, I invoke you all day,
    I stretch out my hands to you:
10 are your marvels meant for the dead,
    can ghosts rise up to praise you?   *Pause*

11 Who talks of your love in the grave,
    of your faithfulness in the place of perdition?[d]
12 Do they hear about your marvels in the dark,
    about your righteousness in the land of oblivion?

13 But I am here, calling for your help,
    praying to you every morning:
14 why do you reject me?
    Why do you hide your face from me?

15 Wretched, slowly dying since my youth,
    I bore your terrors—now I am exhausted;
16 your anger overwhelmed me,
    you destroyed me with your terrors
17 which, like a flood, were round me, all day long,
    all together closing in on me.
18 You have turned my friends and neighbors against me,
    now darkness is my one companion left.

Hymn and a prayer to God's faithfulness[a]

Poem — For Ethan the native-born

1 I will celebrate your love for ever, Yahweh,
  age after age my words shall proclaim your faithfulness;
2 for I claim that love is built to last for ever
  and your faithfulness founded firmly in the heavens.[b]

3 "I have made a covenant with my Chosen,
  I have given my servant David my sworn word:
4 I have founded your dynasty to last for ever,
  I have built you a throne to outlast all time."

Pause

5 Yahweh, the assembly of holy ones in heaven
  applaud the marvel of your faithfulness.
6 Who in the skies can compare with Yahweh?
  Which of the heaven-born[c] can rival him?

7 God, dreaded in the assembly of holy ones,
  great[d] and terrible to all around him,
8 Yahweh, God of Sabaoth, who is like you?—
  mighty Yahweh, clothed in your faithfulness!

9 You control the pride of the ocean,
  when its waves ride high, you calm them;
10 you split Rahab[e] in two like a carcass
  and scattered your enemies with your mighty arm.

11 The heavens are yours and the earth is yours,
  you founded the world and all it holds,
12 you created north and south;
  Tabor and Hermon hail your name with joy.

13 Yours was the arm, and yours the prowess,
  mighty and exalted your right hand;
14 Righteousness and Justice support your throne,
  Love and Faithfulness are your attendants.

15 Happy the people who learn to acclaim you!
  Yahweh, they will live in the light of your favor;
16   they will rejoice in your name all day
    and exult in your righteousness.

17 You are their glory and their strength,
  you, by your kindness, raise our fortunes,*f*
18   since both our shield and our king
    belong to Yahweh, the Holy One of Israel.

19 Once you spoke in vision
  and said to your friends,*g*
  "I have conferred the crown*h* on a hero,
  and promoted one chosen from my people.

20 "I have selected my servant David
  and anointed him with my holy oil;
21   my hand will be constantly with him,
    he will be able to rely on my arm.

22 "No enemy will be able to outwit him,
  no wicked man to worst him,
23   I myself will crush his opponents,
    I will strike dead all who hate him.

24 "With my faithfulness and love,
  his fortunes shall rise in my name.
25   I will give him control of the sea,
    complete control of the rivers.

26 "He will invoke me, 'My father,
  my God and rock of my safety,'
27   and I shall make him my firstborn,
    the Most High*i* for kings on earth.

145

28 "I will keep my love for him always,
my convenant with him shall stand,
29 I have founded his dynasty to last for ever,
his throne to be as lasting as the heavens.

30 "Should his descendants desert my Law
and disregard my rulings,
31 should they violate my statutes
and not keep my commandments,

32 "I will punish their sins with the rod
and their crimes with the whip,
33 but never withdraw my love from him
or fail in my faithfulness.

34 "I will not break my covenant,
I will not revoke my given word;
35 I have sworn on my holiness, once for all,
and cannot turn liar to David.

36 "His dynasty shall last for ever,
I see his throne like the sun,
37 enduring for ever like the moon,
that faithful witness in the sky." *Pause*

38 And yet you have rejected, disowned,
and raged at your anointed;[j]
39 you have repudiated the covenant with your servant
and flung his crown dishonored to the ground.

40 You have pierced all his defenses,
and laid his forts in ruins;
41 anyone may go and loot him,
his neighbors treat him with scorn.

42 You have let his opponents get the upper hand,
and made all his enemies happy,
43 you have snapped his sword on a rock
and failed to support him in battle.

44 You have stripped him of his glorious scepter,
   and toppled his throne to the ground,
45 you have aged him before his time
   and covered him in shame.   *Pause*

46 Yahweh, how much longer will you hide? For ever?
   How much longer must your anger smolder like a fire?
47 Remember me, the short time I have left[k]
   and the void to which you destine mankind.
48 What man can cling to life and not see death?
   Who can evade the clutches of Sheol?   *Pause*

49 Lord, where are those earlier signs of your love?
   You swore your oath to David on your faithfulness!
50 Lord, do not forget how your servant was insulted,
   how I take these pagans' taunts[l] to heart,
51 insults, Yahweh, that your enemies have offered,
   insults to your anointed wherever he goes.

   Blessed be Yahweh for ever.
   Amen. Amen![m]

PSALM 90   V 89

The human condition[a]

Prayer – Of Moses, man of God

1 Lord, you have been
  our refuge[b] age after age.

2 Before the mountains were born,
  before the earth or the world came to birth,
  you were God from all eternity and for ever.

3 You can turn man back into dust
  by saying, "Back to what you were, you sons of men!"

147

⁴   To you, a thousand years are a single day,
     a yesterday now over, an hour of the night.

⁵   You brush men away like waking° dreams,
     they are like grass
⁶   sprouting and flowering in the morning,
     withered and dry before dusk.

⁷   We too are burnt up by your anger
     and terrified by your fury;
⁸   having summoned up our sins
     you inspect our secrets by your own light.

⁹   Our days dwindle under your wrath,
     our lives are over in a breath*ᵈ*
¹⁰   —our life lasts for seventy years,
     eighty with good health,

     but they all add up toᵉ anxiety and trouble—
     over in a trice, and then we are gone.
¹¹   Who yet has felt the full force of your fury,
     or learnt to fear the violence of your rage?ᶠ

¹²   Teach us to count how few days we have
     and so gain wisdom of heart.ᵍ
¹³   Relent, Yahweh! How much longer do we have?
     Take pity on your servants!ʰ

¹⁴   Let us wake in the morning filled with your love
     and sing and be happy all our days;
¹⁵   make our future as happy as our past was sad,
     those years when you were punishing us.

¹⁶   Let your servants see what you can do for them,
     let their children see your glory.
¹⁷   May the sweetness of the Lord be on us!
     Make all we do succeed.ⁱ

PSALM 91

God's protection[a]

1 If you live in the shelter of Elyon
and make your home in the shadow of Shaddai,[b]
2 you can say[c] to Yahweh, "My refuge, my fortress,
my God in whom I trust!"

3 He rescues you from the snares
of fowlers hoping to destroy[d] you;
4a he covers you with his feathers,
4b and you find shelter underneath his wings.

5 You need not fear the terrors of night,
the arrow that flies in the daytime,
6 the plague that stalks in the dark,
the scourge that wreaks havoc in broad daylight.[e]

7 Though a thousand fall at your side,
ten thousand at your right hand,
you yourself will remain unscathed,
4c with his faithfulness for shield and buckler.

8 You have only to look around
to see how the wicked are repaid,
9 you who can say, "Yahweh my refuge,"
and make Elyon your fortress.[f]

10 No disaster can overtake you,
no plague come near your tent:
11 he will put you in his angels' charge
to guard you wherever you go.

12 They will support you on their hands
in case you hurt your foot against a stone;
13 you will tread on lion[g] and adder,
trample on savage lions and dragons.

¹⁴ "I rescue all who cling to me,
 I protect whoever knows my name,
¹⁵ I answer everyone who invokes me,
 I am with them when they are in trouble;
 I bring them safety and honor.
¹⁶ I give them life, long and full,
 and show them how I can save."

PSALM 92 V 91

The virtuous man rejoices

Psalm – Song – For the sabbath

¹ It is good to give thanks to Yahweh,
 to play in honor of your name, Most High,
² to proclaim your love at daybreak
 and your faithfulness all through the night
³ to the music of the zither and lyre,
 to the rippling of the harp.

⁴ I am happy, Yahweh, at what you have done;
 at your achievements I joyfully exclaim,
⁵ "Great are your achievements, Yahweh,
 immensely deep your thoughts!"
⁶ Stupid men are not aware of this,
 fools can never appreciate it.

⁷ The wicked may sprout as thick as weeds
 and every evildoer flourish,
 but only to be everlastingly destroyed,
⁸ whereas you are supreme^a for ever.
⁹ See how your enemies perish,^b
 how all evil men are routed.

10 You raise my horn as if I were a wild ox,
   you pour*c* fresh oil on my head;
11 I was able to see those who were spying on me,*d*
   to overhear what the wicked were whispering,
12 so the virtuous flourish like palm trees
   and grow as tall as the cedars of Lebanon.

13 Planted in the house of Yahweh,
   they will flourish in the courts of our God,
14 still bearing fruit in old age,
   still remaining fresh and green,
15 to proclaim that Yahweh is righteous,
   my rock in whom no fault is to be found!

PSALM 93 V 92

The majesty of God*a*

1 Yahweh is king, robed in majesty,
  Yahweh is robed in power,
  he wears it like a belt.

  You have made the world firm,*b* unshakable;
2 your throne has stood since then,*c*
  you existed from the first, Yahweh.*d*

3 Yahweh, the rivers raise,
  the rivers raise their voices,
  the rivers raise their thunders;

4 greater than the voice of ocean,
  transcending*e* the waves of the sea,
  Yahweh reigns transcendent in the heights.

5 Your decrees*f* will never alter;
  holiness will distinguish your house,*g*
  Yahweh, for ever and ever.

The justice of God[a]

1 Yahweh, God of revenge,
  God of revenge, appear!
2 Rise, judge of the world,
  give the proud their deserts!

3 Yahweh, how much longer are the wicked,
  how much longer are the wicked to triumph?
4 Are these evil men to remain unsilenced,
  boasting and asserting themselves?

5 Yahweh, they crush your people,
  they oppress your hereditary people,
6 murdering and massacring
  widows, orphans, and guests.

7 "Yahweh sees nothing," they say,
  "the God of Jacob takes no notice."
8 You most stupid of men, you fools,
  think this over and learn some sense.

9 Is the inventor of the ear unable to hear?
  The creator of the eye unable to see?
10 The punisher of the pagans unable to punish?
  Yahweh the teacher of mankind
11 knows exactly how men think,
  how their thoughts are a puff of wind.

12 Yahweh, happy the man whom you instruct,
  the man whom you teach through your law;[b]
13 his mind is at peace though times are bad,
  while a pit is being dug for the wicked.

14 For Yahweh has not abandoned
   or deserted his hereditary people;
15 for verdict will return to righteousness again,
   and, in its wake, all upright hearts.

16 No one ever stood up for me against the wicked,
   not a soul took a stand to save me from evil men;
17 without Yahweh's help, I should, long ago,
   have gone to the Home of Silence.[c]

18 I need only say, "I am slipping,"
   and your love, Yahweh, immediately supports me;
19 and in the middle of all my troubles
   you console me and make me happy.

20 You never consent to that corrupt tribunal
   that imposes disorder as law,
21 that takes the life of the virtuous
   and condemns the innocent to death.

22 No! Yahweh is still my citadel,
   my God is a rock where I take shelter;
23 he will pay them back for all their sins,
   he will silence their wickedness,
   Yahweh our God will silence them.

PSALM 95   V 94

Psalm for daily use

1 Come, let us praise Yahweh joyfully,
   acclaiming the Rock[a] of our safety;
2 let us come into his presence with thanksgiving,
   acclaiming him with music.

3 For Yahweh is a great God,
   a greater King than all other gods;

4   from depths of earth to mountaintop
    everything comes under his rule;
5   the sea belongs to him, he made it,
    so does the land, he shaped this too.

6   Come in, let us bow, prostrate ourselves,
    and kneel in front of Yahweh our maker,
7   for this is our God,
    and we are the people he pastures,
    the flock that he guides.[b]

    If only you would listen to him today,
8   "Do not harden your hearts as at Meribah,
    as you did that day at Massah in the wilderness,[c]
9   when your ancestors challenged me, tested me,
    although they had seen what I could do.

10 "For forty years that[d] generation repelled me,
    until I said: How unreliable these people
    who refuse to grasp my ways!
11 And so, in anger, I swore that not one
    would reach the place of rest I had for them."

PSALM 96

Yahweh, king and judge[a]

1   Sing Yahweh a new song!
    Sing to Yahweh, all the earth!
2   Sing to Yahweh, bless his name.

    Proclaim his salvation day after day,
3   tell of his glory among the nations,
    tell his marvels to every people.

4   Yahweh is great, loud must be his praise,
    he is to be feared beyond all gods.
5   Nothingness, all the gods of the nations.[b]

154

Yahweh himself made the heavens,
6 in his presence are splendor and majesty,
in his sanctuary power and beauty.

7 Pay tribute to Yahweh, families of the peoples,
tribute to Yahweh of glory and power,
8 tribute to Yahweh of his name's due glory.[c]

Bring out the offering, bear it[d] before him,
9 worship Yahweh in his sacred court,[e]
tremble before him, all the earth!

10 Say among the nations, "Yahweh is king!"
Firm has he made the world, and unshakable;
he will judge each nation with strict justice.

11 Let the heavens be glad, let earth rejoice,
let the sea thunder and all that it holds,
12 let the fields exult and all that is in them,
let all the woodland trees cry out for joy,

13 at the presence of Yahweh, for he comes,
he comes to judge the earth,
to judge the world with justice
and the nations with his truth.

PSALM 97   V 96

The triumph of Yahweh[a]

1 Yahweh is king! Let earth rejoice,
the many isles be glad!
2 Cloud and Darkness surround him,
Righteousness and Justice support his throne.

3 A fire precedes him as he goes,
devouring all enemies around him;
4 his lightning lights up the world,
earth observes and quakes.

5 The mountains melt like wax[b]
   at the coming of the Master of the world;
6 the heavens proclaim his righteousness,
   all nations see his glory.

7 Shame on those who worship images,
   who take pride in their idols:
   bow down as he passes, all you gods!

8 Zion hears and rejoices,
   the daughters of Judah[c] exult
   at the rulings you utter, Yahweh.

9 For you are Yahweh
   Most High over the world,
   far transcending all other gods.

10 Yahweh loves those who repudiate[d] evil,
   he guards the souls of the devout,
   rescuing them from the clutches of the wicked.

11 Light dawns[e] for the virtuous,
   and joy, for upright hearts.
12 Rejoice in Yahweh, you virtuous,
   remember his holiness, and praise him!

PSALM 98   V 97

The judge of the world[a]

Psalm

1 Sing Yahweh a new song
   for he has performed marvels,
   his own right hand, his holy arm,
   gives him the power to save.

[2] Yahweh has displayed his power;
    has revealed his righteousness to the nations,
[3] mindful of his love and faithfulness
        to the House of Israel.

The most distant parts of the earth have seen
    the saving power of our God.
[4] Acclaim Yahweh, all the earth,
    burst into shouts of joy![b]

[5] Sing to Yahweh, sing to the music of harps,
    and to the sound of many instruments;
[6] to the sound of trumpet and horn[c]
    acclaim Yahweh the King!

[7] Let the sea thunder and all that it holds,
    and the world, with all who live in it;
[8] let all the rivers clap their hands
    and the mountains shout for joy,

[9] at the presence of Yahweh, for he comes
        to judge the earth,
    to judge the world with righteousness
    and the nations with strict justice.

PSALM 99 V 98

God, righteous and holy king[a]

[1] Yahweh is king, the nations tremble;
    he is enthroned on the cherubs, earth quakes;
[2]   Yahweh is great in Zion.

He is high over all nations;
[3] may they praise your great and terrible name,
[4]   "Holy is he, and mighty!"[b]

You are a king who loves justice,
insisting on honesty, justice, virtue,
   as you have done for Jacob.

5 Let us extol Yahweh our God,
and worship at his footstool,
   "Holy is he!"

6 Moses, Aaron one of his priests, and Samuel[c]
his votary, all invoked Yahweh:
   and he answered them.

7 He talked with them in the pillar of cloud;
they obeyed his decrees, the Law he gave them.

8 Yahweh our God, you responded to them,
a God of forgiveness for them,
   in spite of punishing their sins.

9 Extol Yahweh our God,
worship at his holy mountain,
   "Holy is Yahweh our God!"

PSALM 100   V 99

Invitation to praise God

Psalm – For thanksgiving

1 Acclaim Yahweh, all the earth,
2 serve Yahweh gladly,
come into his presence with songs of joy!

3 Know that he, Yahweh, is God,
he made us and we belong to him,
we are his people, the flock that he pastures.

⁴ Walk through his porticos giving thanks,
   enter his courts praising him,
   give thanks to him, bless his name!

⁵ Yes, Yahweh is good,ᵃ
   his love is everlasting,ᵇ
   his faithfulness endures from age to age.

PSALM 101

The ideal rulerᵃ

Of David – Psalm

¹ My song is about kindness and justice;
   Yahweh, I sing it to you.
² I mean to make good progress, as the blameless do;
   when will you come to me?ᵇ

   In my household, I will advance
      in purity of heart;
³ I will not let my eyes rest
      on any misconduct.

   I hate the practices of the apostate,
      they have no appeal for me;
⁴ perverted hearts must keep their distance,
      the wicked I disregard.

⁵ The man who secretly slanders his neighbor
      I reduce to silence;
   haughty looks, proud heart,
      I cannot tolerate these.

⁶ I look to my religious countrymen
      to compose my household;
   only the man who makes progress, as the blameless do,
      can be my servant.

7 There is no room in my house
  for any hypocrite;
no liar keeps his post
  where I can see him.

8 Morning after morning[c] I reduce to silence
all who are wicked in this country,
banishing from the city of Yahweh
all evil men.

PSALM 102

Prayer in misfortune[a]

*Prayer of the downtrodden telling Yahweh their troubles at a
moment of distress*

1 Yahweh, hear my prayer,
  let my cry for help reach you;
2 do not hide your face from me
  when I am in trouble;
  bend down to listen to me,
  when I call, be quick to answer me!

3 For my days are vanishing like smoke,
  my bones smoldering like logs,
4 my heart shriveling like scorched grass
  and my appetite has gone;
5 whenever I heave a sigh,
  my bones stick through my skin.

6 I live in a desert like the pelican,
  in a ruin like the screech owl,
7 I stay awake, lamenting[b]
  like a lone bird on the roof;
8 my enemies insult me all day long,
  those who used to praise me[c] now use me as a curse.[d]

160

9   Ashes are the bread I eat,
        what I drink I lace with tears,
10   under your furious anger,
        since you only picked me up to throw me down;
11   my days dwindle away like a shadow,
        I am as dry as hay.

12 Whereas, Yahweh, you remain for ever;
        each generation in turn remembers you!

13 Rise, take pity on Zion!—
        the time has come to have mercy on her,
        the hour has come;
14 for your servants prize her stones
        and are moved to pity by her dust.

15 Then will the nations fear the name of Yahweh
        and all kings on earth respect your glory;
16 when Yahweh builds Zion anew,
        he will be seen in his glory;
17 he will answer the prayer of the abandoned,
        he will not scorn their petitions.

18 Put this on record for the next generation,
        so that a race still to be born can praise God: [e]
19 Yahweh has leaned down from the heights of his sanc-
            tuary,
        has looked down at earth from heaven,
20 to hear the sighing of the captive,
        and to set free those doomed to die.

28 Your servants' sons will have a permanent home,
        and their descendants be in your presence always,
21 to proclaim the name of Yahweh in Zion,
        his praise in Jerusalem;
22 nations and kingdoms will be united
        and offer worship to Yahweh together.

23a My strength has already run out; [f]
24a tell me how much longer I have left. [g]
23b
24b Do not take me prematurely,
        when your own life lasts for ever.

25   Aeons ago, you laid earth's foundations,
      the heavens are the work of your hands;
26   all will vanish, though you remain,
      all wear out like a garment,
      like clothes that need changing you will change them;
27   but yourself, you never change,[h] and your years are
      unending.

PSALM 103

God is love

Of David

1   Bless Yahweh, my soul,
     bless his holy name, all that is in me!
2   Bless Yahweh, my soul,
     and remember all his kindnesses:

3   in forgiving all your offenses,
     in curing all your diseases,
4   in redeeming your life from the Pit,
     in crowning you with love and tenderness,
5   in filling your years[a] with prosperity,
     in renewing your youth like an eagle's.[b]

6   Yahweh, who does what is right,
     is always on the side of the oppressed;

7   he revealed his intentions to Moses,
     his prowess to the sons of Israel.

8   Yahweh is tender and compassionate,
     slow to anger, most loving;[c]
9   his indignation does not last for ever,
     his resentment exists a short time only;

10 he never treats us, never punishes us,
as our guilt and our sins deserve.

11 No less than the height of heaven over earth
is the greatness of his love for those who fear him;
12 he takes our sins farther away
than the east is from the west.

13 As tenderly as a father treats his children,
so Yahweh treats those who fear him;
14 he knows what we are made of,
he remembers we are dust.

15 Man lasts no longer than grass,
no longer than a wild flower he lives,
16 one gust of wind, and he is gone,
never to be seen there again;

17 yet Yahweh's love for those who fear him
lasts from all eternity and for ever,
like his goodness to their children's children,
18 as long as they keep his covenant
and remember to obey his precepts.

19 Yahweh has fixed his throne in the heavens,
his empire is over all.
20 Bless Yahweh, all his angels,
heroes mighty to enforce his word,
attentive to his word of command.

21 Bless Yahweh, all his armies,
servants to enforce his will.
22 Bless Yahweh, all his creatures
in every part of his empire!

Bless Yahweh, my soul.

The glories of creation[a]

1 Bless Yahweh, my soul.
   Yahweh my God, how great you are!
   Clothed in majesty and glory,
2 wrapped in a robe of light!

   You stretch the heavens out like a tent,
3 you build your palace on the waters above;
   using the clouds as your chariot,
   you advance on the wings of the wind;
4 you use the winds as messengers
   and fiery flames as servants.

5 You fixed the earth on its foundations,
   unshakable for ever and ever;
6 you wrapped it with the deep as with a robe,
   the waters overtopping the mountains.

7 At your reproof the waters took to flight,
   they fled at the sound of your thunder,
8 cascading over the mountains, into the valleys,
   down to the reservoir you made for them;
9 you imposed the limits they must never cross again,
   or they would once more flood the land.

10 You set springs gushing in ravines,
   running down between the mountains,
11 supplying water for wild animals,
   attracting the thirsty wild donkeys;[b]
12 near there the birds of the air make their nests
   and sing among the branches.

13 From your palace you water the uplands
    until the ground has had all that your heavens have to
        offer;*c*
14 you make fresh grass grow for cattle
    and those plants made use of by man,
    for them to get food from the soil:
15 wine to make them cheerful,
    oil to make them happy
    and bread to make them strong.

16 The trees of Yahweh get rain enough,
    those cedars of Lebanon he planted;
17 here the little birds build their nest
    and, on the highest branches,*d* the stork has its home.
18 For the wild goats there are the mountains,
    in the crags rock badgers*e* hide.

19 You made the moon to tell the seasons,
    the sun knows when to set:
20 you bring darkness on, night falls,
    all the forest animals come out:
21 savage lions roaring for their prey,
    claiming their food from God.

22 The sun rises, they retire,
    going back to lie down in their lairs,
23 and man goes out to work,
    and to labor until dusk.
24 Yahweh, what variety you have created,
    arranging everything so wisely!
    Earth is completely full of things you have made:

25 among them vast expanse of ocean,
    teeming with countless creatures,
    creatures large and small,
26 with the ships going to and fro
    and Leviathan whom you made to amuse you.

27 All creatures depend on you
    to feed them throughout the year;

28 you provide the food they eat,
    with generous hand you satisfy their hunger.

29 You turn your face away, they suffer,
    you stop their breath, they die
    and revert to dust.
30 You give breath, fresh life begins,*f*
    you keep renewing the world.

31 Glory for ever to Yahweh!
    May Yahweh find joy in what he creates,
32 at whose glance the earth trembles,
    at whose touch the mountains smoke!

33 I mean to sing to Yahweh all my life,
    I mean to play for my God as long as I live.
34 May these reflections of mine give him pleasure,
    as much as Yahweh gives me!
35 May sinners vanish from the earth
    and the wicked exist no more!

    Bless Yahweh, my soul.*g*

PSALM 105   V 104

The wonderful history of Israel*a*

Alleluia!

1 Give thanks to Yahweh, call his name aloud,
   proclaim his deeds to the peoples!
2 Sing to him, play to him,
   tell over all his marvels!
3 Glory in his holy name,
   let the hearts that seek Yahweh rejoice!

4 Seek Yahweh and his strength,
  seek his face untiringly;
5 remember the marvels he has done,
  his wonders, the judgments from his mouth.

6 Stock of Abraham his servant,
  sons of Jacob his chosen one![b]
7 He is Yahweh our God,
  his authority is over all the earth.

8 Remember his covenant for ever,
  his word of command for a thousand generations,
9 the pact he made with Abraham,
  his oath to Isaac.

10 He established it as a statute for Jacob,
   an everlasting covenant for Israel.
11 "I give you a land," he said,
   "Canaan, your allotted heritage.

12 "There where you were easily counted,
   few in number, strangers to the country."
13 They went from nation to nation,
   from one kingdom to another people;

14 he let no man oppress them,
   he punished kings on their behalf.
15 "Do not touch my anointed ones," he said,
   "do not harm my prophets!"

16 Next, he called down famine on the country,
   he broke their staff, that is, their bread;[c]
17 he sent a man ahead of them,
   Joseph, sold as a slave.

18 They tortured his feet with fetters,
   they put his neck in irons;
19 time passed, Joseph's oracle came true,
   Yahweh's word proved him right.

²⁰ The king gave orders to release him,
that master of nations set him free,
²¹ putting him in charge of his household,
in control of all he possessed,

²² to train^d his officials as he thought fit
and convert his elders into sages.
²³ Israel then migrated to Egypt,
Jacob settled in the land of Ham.

²⁴ He made his people fertile
and more vigorous than their oppressors,
²⁵ whose hearts he then disposed to hatred of his people
and double-dealing with his servants.

²⁶ He sent his servant Moses,
and Aaron, the man of his choice;
²⁷ there they displayed^e his signs,
his wonders in the land of Ham.

²⁸ He sent darkness, darkness fell,
but still they defied^f his word.
²⁹ He turned their rivers into blood,
thus killing all their fish.

³⁰ Their country was overrun with frogs
even in the royal apartments;
³¹ he spoke: flies and mosquitoes
swarmed throughout the country.

³² He sent them hail instead of rain,
fire swept across their land;
³³ he blasted their vines and fig trees,
he shattered the trees throughout the country.

³⁴ he spoke: there came locusts,
grasshoppers, more than you could count,
³⁵ eating every scrap of greenstuff,
every blade their soil produced.

[36] Next, he struck down all the firstborn in their land,
the entire first fruits of their fertility;
[37] then he led Israel out with gold and silver,
and not one man of their tribes was left behind.

[38] Egypt was glad to see them go,
they had filled her with alarm;
[39] he spread a cloud to cover them,
and a fire to glow at night.

[40] They demanded food, he sent them quails,
he satisfied them with the bread of heaven;
[41] he opened the rock, the waters gushed
to flow through the desert like a river.

[42] Yes, faithful to the sacred promise
given to his servant Abraham,
[43] he led his happy people forward,
to joyful shouts from his chosen,

[44] and gave them the pagans' territories.
Where others had toiled, they took possession,
[45] on condition that they kept his statutes
and remained obedient to his laws.

PSALM 106 V 105

National confession[a]

Alleluia!

[1] Give thanks to Yahweh, for he is good,
his love is everlasting!
[2] Who can count all Yahweh's triumphs?
Who can praise him enough?

[3] Happy are we if we exercise justice
and constantly practice virtue!

4 Yahweh, remember me,
  for the love you bear your people,
  come to me as a savior,
5 let me share the happiness of your chosen,
  the joys of your nation
  and take pride in being one of your heirs.

6 We have sinned quite as much as our fathers,
  we have been wicked, we are guilty;
7 our ancestors in Egypt never grasped
  the meaning of your marvels.

  They failed to appreciate your great love,
  they defied the Most High[b] at the Sea of Reeds.
8 For the sake of his name, he saved them
  to demonstrate his power.

9 One word from him dried up the Sea of Reeds,
  he led them across the sea bed like dry land,
10 he saved them from the grasp of those who hated them
  and rescued them from the clutches of the enemy.

11 And the waters swallowed their oppressors,
  not one of them was left.
12 Then, having faith in his promises,
  they immediately sang his praises.

13 They forgot his achievements as quickly,
  going on before asking his advice;
14 their desires overcame them in the desert,
  they challenged God in the wilds.

15 He granted them what they asked for,
  then struck them with a wasting fever;[c]
16 in camp, they grew jealous of Moses
  and Aaron, Yahweh's holy one.

17 The earth opened, swallowing Dathan,
  closing on Abiram's faction,
18 fire flamed out against their faction,
  the renegades went up in flames.

19 They made a calf at Horeb,
    performed prostrations to a smelted thing,
20 exchanging the one who was their glory
    for the image of a grass-eating ox.

21 They forgot the God who had saved them
    by performing such feats in Egypt,
22 such wonders in the land of Ham,
    such fearful things at the Sea of Reeds.

23 He talked of putting an end to them
    and would have done, if Moses his chosen
    had not stood in the breach, confronting him,
    and deflecting his destructive anger.

24 They refused a land of delight,
    having no faith in his promise;
25 they stayed in their camp and grumbled,
    they would not listen to Yahweh's voice.

26 So, raising his hand, he swore
    to make them fall dead in the desert
27 and their descendants to fall to the heathen,
    and to disperse them throughout those countries.

28 They accepted the yoke of Baal-peor
    and ate sacrifices to the dead.
29 They provoked him by their behavior;
    plague broke out among them.

30 Then up stood Phinehas to intervene,
    and the plague was checked;
31 hence his reputation for virtue
    through successive generations for ever.

32 They enraged him at the waters of Meribah;
    as a result, things went wrong for Moses,
33 since they had embittered[d] his spirit
    and he spoke without stopping to think.

34 They did not destroy the pagans
   as Yahweh had told them to do,
35 but, intermarrying with them,
   adopted their practices instead.

36 Serving the pagans' idols,
   they found themselves trapped
37 into sacrificing their own sons
   and daughters to demons.

38 They shed innocent blood,
   the blood of their sons and daughters,
   offering them to the idols of Canaan,
   they polluted the country with blood.

39 They defiled themselves by such actions,
   their behavior was that of a whore.[e]
40 Yahweh's anger blazed out at his people,
   he came to loathe his heirs.

41 He handed them over to the pagans,
   those who hated them became their masters;
42 their enemies tyrannized over them,
   crushing them under their rule.

43 Time and again he rescued them,
   but they went on defying him deliberately
   and plunging deeper into wickedness;
44 even so, he took pity on their distress
   each time he heard them calling.

45 For their sake, he remembered his covenant,
   he relented in his great love,
46 making their captors mitigate
   the harshness of their treatment.

47 Yahweh our God and savior,
   gather us from among the pagans,
   to give thanks to your holy name
   and to find our happiness in praising you.

[48] Blessed be Yahweh the God of Israel,
from all eternity and for ever!
Here, all the people are to say, "Amen."[f]

PSALM 107 V 106

God, a refuge in all dangers[a]

Alleluia!

[1] Give thanks to Yahweh, for he is good,
his love is everlasting:
[2] let these be the words of Yahweh's redeemed,
those he has redeemed from the oppressor's clutches,
[3] by bringing them home from foreign countries,
from east and west, from north and south.[b]

[4] Some had lost their way in the wilds and the desert,
not knowing how to reach an inhabited town;
[5] they were hungry and desperately thirsty,
their courage was running low.

[6] Then they called to Yahweh in their trouble
and he rescued them from their sufferings,
[7] guiding them by a route leading
direct to an inhabited town.[c]

[8] Let these thank Yahweh for his love,
for his marvels on behalf of men;
[9] satisfying the hungry,
he fills the starving with good things.

[10] Some were living in gloom and darkness,
fettered in misery and irons
[11] for defying the orders of God,
for scorning the advice of the Most High;
[12] who bent them double with hardship,
to breaking point, with no one to help them.

13 Then they called to Yahweh in their trouble
and he rescued them from their sufferings;
14 releasing them from gloom and darkness,
shattering their chains.

15 Let these thank Yahweh for his love,
for his marvels on behalf of men;
16 breaking bronze gates open,
he smashes iron bars.

17 Some, driven frantic by their sins,
made miserable by their own guilt
18 and finding all food repugnant,
were nearly at death's door.

19 Then they called to Yahweh in their trouble
and he rescued them from their sufferings;
20 sending his word and curing them,
he snatched them from the Pit.[a]

21 Let these thank Yahweh for his love,
for his marvels on behalf of men.
22 Let them offer thanksgiving sacrifices
and proclaim with shouts of joy what he has done.

23 Others, taking ship and going to sea,
were plying their business across the ocean;
24 they too saw what Yahweh could do,
what marvels on the deep!

25 He spoke and raised a gale,
lashing up towering waves.
26 Flung to the sky, then plunged to the depths,
they lost their nerve in the ordeal,
27 staggering and reeling like drunkards
with all their seamanship adrift.

28 Then they called to Yahweh in their trouble
and he rescued them from their sufferings,
29 reducing the storm to a whisper
until the waves grew quiet,

30 bringing them, glad at the calm,
   safe to the port they were bound for.

31 Let these thank Yahweh for his love,
   for his marvels on behalf of men.
32 Let them extol him at the Great Assembly
   and praise him in the Council of Elders.

33 Sometimes he turned rivers into desert,
   springs of water into arid ground,
34 or a fertile country into salt flats,
   because the people living there were wicked.

35 Or again, he turned a desert into sheets of water,
   and an arid country into flowing springs,
36 where he gave the hungry a home
   in which to found a habitable town.

37 There, they sow the fields and plant their vines,
   there, they show a profitable harvest.
38 He blesses them, they grow in number,
   he sees that their livestock does not decrease.

39 Their numbers had fallen, they had grown weak
   under pressure of disaster and hardship.
40 Pouring his contempt upon the nobly born,
   he left them to wander in a trackless waste.

41 But now, he lifts the needy out of their misery,
   and gives them a flock of new families;
42 at the sight of which, upright hearts rejoice
   and wickedness must hold its tongue.

43 If you are wise, study these things
   and realize how Yahweh shows his love.

PSALM 108

Morning hymn and national prayer[a]

Song – Psalm – Of David

1 My heart is ready, God
  —I mean to sing and play.
  Awake, my muse,
2 awake, lyre and harp,
  I mean to wake the Dawn!

3 Yahweh, I mean to thank you among the peoples,
  to play music to you among the nations;
4 your love is high as heaven,
  your faithfulness as the clouds.
5 Rise high above the heavens, God,
  let your glory be over the earth!

6 To bring rescue to those you love
  save with your right hand and answer us!

7 God promised us once from his sanctuary,
  "I the Victor will parcel out Shechem,
  and share out the Valley of Succoth.

8 "Gilead is mine, Manasseh mine,
  Ephraim is my helmet,
  Judah, my marshal's baton.

9 "Moab a bowl for me to wash in!
  I throw my sandal over Edom
  and shout: Victory! over Philistia."

10 Who is there now to take me into the fortified city,
  to lead me into Edom?

11 God, can you really have rejected us?
You no longer march with our armies.

12 Help us in this hour of crisis,
the help that man can give is worthless.
13 With God among us, we shall fight like heroes,
he will trample on our enemies.

PSALM 109 V 108

An appeal against enemies[a]

For the choirmaster – Of David – Psalm

1 God whom I praise, break your silence,
2 now that the wicked and the false
are both accusing me.
They are defaming me,
3 saying malicious things about me,
attacking me for no reason.

4 In return for my friendship, they denounce me,
though all I had done was pray for them;[b]
5 they pay me back evil for kindness
and hatred for friendship.

6 "Give him a venal judge,
find someone to frame the charge;[c]
7 let him be tried and found guilty,
let his prayer be construed as a crime!

8 "Let his life be cut short,
let someone else take his office;
9 may his children be orphaned
and his wife widowed!

10 "May his children be homeless vagabonds,
　　beggared and hounded from[d] their hovels;
11 may the creditor seize his possessions
　　and foreigners swallow his profits!

12 "May no one be left to show him kindness,
　　may no one look after his orphans,
13 may his family die out,
　　its name disappear in one generation!

14 "May the crimes of his fathers be held against him[e]
　　and his mother's sin never be effaced;
15 may Yahweh bear these constantly in mind,
　　to wipe their memory off the earth!"

16 That wretch never thought of being kind,
　　but hounded the poor, the needy
　　and the brokenhearted to death.
17 He loved cursing, may it recoil on him,
　　had no taste for blessing, may it shun him![f]

18 He used to wrap curses round him like a cloak,
　　let them soak right into him like water,[g]
　　deep into his bones like oil.
19 May they now envelop him like a gown,
　　be tied round his waist for ever!

20 May Yahweh pay all my accusers,
　　all my detractors like this!
21 Yahweh, defend me for the sake of your name,
　　rescue me, since your love is generous!

22 Reduced to weakness and poverty,
　　my heart is sorely tormented;[h]
23 I am dwindling away like a shadow,
　　they have brushed me off like a locust.[i]

24 My knees are weak for lack of food,
　　my body is thin for lack of oil;
25 I have become an object of derision,
　　people shake their heads at me in scorn.

²⁶ Help me, Yahweh my God,
save me since you love me,
²⁷ and let them know that you have done it,
that it was you, Yahweh, who did it.

²⁸ Counter their curses with your blessing,
shame my aggressors, make your servant glad!
²⁹ Clothe my accusers in disgrace,
cover them with a cloak of shame.

³⁰ I will give thanks aloud to Yahweh
and praise him in the Assembly,
³¹ for conducting the poor man's defense
against those who would have sentenced him to death.

PSALM 110   V 109

The Messiah: king and priest[a]

Of David – Psalm

¹ Yahweh's oracle to you, my Lord, "Sit at my right hand[b]
and I will make your enemies a footstool[c] for you."

² Yahweh will force all your enemies
under the sway of your scepter in Zion.

³ Royal dignity was yours from the day you were born, on
the holy mountains,[d]
royal from the womb, from the dawn of your earliest
days.[e]

⁴ Yahweh has sworn an oath which he never will retract,
"You are a priest of the order of Melchizedek, and for
ever."

⁵ The Lord is at your right hand.[f]
When he grows angry he shatters[g] kings,

6 he gives the nations their deserts,
   smashing their skulls, he heaps the wide world with
       corpses.[h]
7 Drinking from the stream as he goes,[i]
   he can hold his head high in victory.[j]

PSALM 111

In praise of the divine attributes[a]

1 Alleluia!

   Aleph I give thanks to Yahweh with all my heart
   Beth where the virtuous meet and the people assemble.
2 *Ghimel* The works of Yahweh are sublime,
   Daleth those who delight in them are right to fix their
       eyes on them.

3 *He* Every work that he does is full of glory and majesty,
   Wau and his righteousness can never change.

4 *Zain* He allows us to commemorate his marvels.[b]
   Heth Yahweh is merciful and tenderhearted,

5 *Teth* he provides food for those who fear him;[c]
   Yod he never forgets his covenant.

6 *Kaph* He reminds his people of the power that he
       wields
   Lamed by giving them the inheritance of the nations.

7 *Mem* All that he does is done in faithfulness and
       justice,
   Nun in all ways his precepts are dependable,

8 *Samek* ordained to last for ever and ever,
   Ain framed in faithfulness and integrity.

⁹ *Pe*　Quickly he comes to his people's rescue,
Sade　imposing his covenant once and for all;
Qoph　so holy his name, commanding our dread.

¹⁰ *Resh*　This fear of Yahweh is the beginning of wisdom,
Shin　they have sound sense who practice it.
Tau　His praises will be sung for ever.

PSALM 112　　　V *111*

In praise of the virtuous^a

¹ Alleluia!

Aleph　Happy the man who fears Yahweh
Beth　by joyfully keeping his commandments!

² *Ghimel*　Children of such a man will be powers on
earth,
Daleth　descendants of the upright will always be
blessed.

³ *He*　There will be riches and wealth for his family,
Wau　and his righteousness^b can never change.

⁴ *Zain*　For the upright he shines^c like a lamp in the dark,
he is merciful, tenderhearted, virtuous.

⁵ *Teth*　Interest is not charged by this good man,
Yod　he is honest in all his dealings.

⁶ *Kaph*　Kept safe by virtue, he is ever steadfast,
Lamed　and leaves an imperishable memory behind
him;

⁷ *Mem*　with constant heart, and confidence in Yahweh,
Nun　he need never fear bad news.

8 *Samek* Steadfast in heart he overcomes his fears:
   Ain in the end he will triumph over his enemies.

9 *Pe* Quick to be generous, he gives to the poor,
   Sade his righteousness can never change,
   Qoph men such as this will always be honored,[d]

10 *Resh* though this fills the wicked with fury
    Shin until, grinding their teeth, they waste away,
    Tau vanishing like their vain hopes.

PSALM 113   V *112*

To God the glorious, the merciful[a]

1 Alleluia!

  You servants of Yahweh, praise,
  praise the name of Yahweh!
2 Blessed be the name of Yahweh,
  henceforth and for ever!
3 From east to west,
  praised be the name of Yahweh!

4 High over all nations, Yahweh!
  His glory transcends the heavens!
5 Who is like Yahweh our God?—
  enthroned so high, he needs to stoop
6 to see the sky and earth!

7 He raises the poor from the dust;
  he lifts the needy from the dunghill
8 to give them a place with princes,
  with the princes of his people.
9 He enthrones the barren woman in her house
  by making her the happy mother[b] of sons.

PSALM 114

Hymn for the Passover[a]

Alleluia![b]

1 When Israel came out of Egypt,
   the House of Jacob from a foreign nation,
2 Judah became his sanctuary
   and Israel his domain.

3 The sea fled at the sight,
   the Jordan stopped flowing,
4 the mountains skipped like rams,
   and like lambs, the hills.

5 Sea, what makes you run away?
   Jordan, why stop flowing?
6 Why skip like rams, you mountains,
   why like lambs, you hills?

7 Quake, earth, at the coming of your Master,
   at the coming of the God of Jacob,
8 who turns rock into pool
   flint into fountain.

PSALM 115

The one true God

1 Not by us, Yahweh, not by us,
   by you alone is glory deserved,
   by your love and your faithfulness!
2 Do the pagans ask, "Where is their God?"

3 Ours is the God whose will is sovereign
  in the heavens and on earth,[a]
4 whereas their idols, in silver and gold,
  products of human skill,

5 have mouths, but never speak,
  eyes, but never see,
6 ears, but never hear,
  noses, but never smell,

7 hands, but never touch,
  feet, but never walk,
  and not a sound from their throats.
8 Their makers will end up like them,
  and so will anyone who relies on them.

9 House of Israel, rely on Yahweh,
  on him, our help and shield!
10 House of Aaron, rely on Yahweh,
  on him, our help and shield!
11 You who fear Yahweh, rely on Yahweh,
  on him, our help and shield![b]

12 Yahweh remembers us, he will bless,[c]
  he will bless the House of Israel,
  he will bless the House of Aaron,
13 he will bless those who fear Yahweh,
  without distinction of rank.

14 May Yahweh add to your numbers,
  yours and your children's too!
15 May you be blessed by Yahweh,
  maker of heaven and earth!
16 Heaven belongs to Yahweh,
  earth he bestows on man.

17 The dead cannot praise Yahweh,
  they have gone down to silence;
18 but we, the living, bless Yahweh
  henceforth and evermore.

Thanksgiving

Alleluia![a]

1 I love! For Yahweh listens
    to my entreaty;
2 he bends down to listen to me
    when[b] I call.

3 Death's cords were tightening round me,
    the nooses[c] of Sheol;
    distress and anguish gripped me,
4   I invoked the name of Yahweh:

"Yahweh, rescue me!"

5 Yahweh is righteous and merciful,
    our God is tenderhearted;
6 Yahweh defends the simple,
    he saved me when I was brought to my knees.

7 Return to your resting place, my soul,
    Yahweh has treated you kindly.
8 He has[d] rescued (me from death) my eyes from tears
    and my feet from stumbling.

9 (I will walk in Yahweh's presence
    in the land of the living.)[e]

10 I have faith, even when I say,
    "I am completely crushed."
11 In my alarm, I declared,
    "No man can be relied on."

12 What return can I make to Yahweh
    for all his goodness to me?

13 I will offer libations to my savior,
    invoking the name of Yahweh.[f]

14 (I will pay what I vowed to Yahweh;
    may his whole nation be present!)

15 The death of the devout
    costs Yahweh dear.[g]
16 Yahweh, I am your servant,
    your servant, son of a pious mother,
    you undo my fetters.

17 I will offer you the thanksgiving sacrifice,
    invoking the name of Yahweh.
 9 I will walk in Yahweh's presence
    in the land of the living.

18 I will pay what I vowed to Yahweh;
    may his whole nation be present,
19 in the courts of the house of Yahweh,
    in your heart, Jerusalem.

PSALM 117   V 116

Summons to praise

Alleluia![a]

1 Praise Yahweh, all nations,
    extol him, all you peoples!
2 For his love is strong,
    his faithfulness eternal.

Processional hymn for the feast of Tabernacles[a]

Alleluia![b]

1   Give thanks to Yahweh, for he is good,
        his love is everlasting!
2   Let the House[c] of Israel say it,
        "His love is everlasting!"

3   Let the House of Aaron say it,
        "His love is everlasting!"
4   Let those who fear Yahweh say it,
        "His love is everlasting!"

5   Hard pressed, I invoked Yahweh,
        he heard me and came to my relief.
6   With Yahweh on my side, I fear nothing:
        what can man do to me?
7   With Yahweh on my side, best help of all,
        I can triumph over my enemies.

8   I would rather take refuge in Yahweh
        than rely on men;
9   I would rather take refuge in Yahweh
        than rely on princes.

10 The pagans were swarming round me,
        in the name of Yahweh I cut them down;[d]
11 they swarmed round me closer and closer,
        in the name of Yahweh I cut them down;

12 they swarmed round me like bees,
        they blazed[e] like a thorn fire,
        in the name of Yahweh I cut them down.

13 I was pressed,[f] pressed, about to fall,
      but Yahweh came to my help;
14 Yahweh is my strength and my song,
      he has been my savior.

15 Shouts of joy and safety
      in the tents of the virtuous:
   Yahweh's right hand is wreaking havoc,[g]
16   Yahweh's right hand is winning,
   Yahweh's right hand is wreaking havoc!

17 No, I shall not die, I shall live
      to recite the deeds of Yahweh;
18 though Yahweh has punished me often,
      he has not abandoned me to Death.

19 Open the gates of virtue to me,
      I will come in and give thanks to Yahweh.
20 This is Yahweh's gateway,
      through which the virtuous may enter.
21 I thank you for having heard me,
      you have been my savior.

22 It was the stone rejected by the builders
      that proved to be the keystone;
23 this is Yahweh's doing
      and it is wonderful to see.[h]
24 This is the day made memorable by Yahweh,
      what immense joy for us![i]

25 Please, Yahweh, please save us.[j]
   Please, Yahweh, please give us prosperity.
26 Blessings on him who comes in the name of Yahweh!
   We bless you from the house of Yahweh.
27 Yahweh is God, he smiles on us.
   With branches in your hands draw up in procession
      as far as the horns of the altar,[k]

²⁸ You are my God, I give you thanks,
    I extol you, my God;
I give you thanks for having heard me,
    you have been my savior.
²⁹ Give thanks to Yahweh, for he is good,
    his love is everlasting!

PSALM 119 V *118*

In praise of the divine Law[a]

¹ *Aleph* Ah, how happy those of blameless life
    who walk in the Law of Yahweh!
² How happy those who respect his decrees,
    and seek him with their whole heart,
³ and, doing no evil,
    walk in his ways!
⁴ You yourself have made your precepts known,
    to be faithfully kept.
⁵ Oh, may my behavior be constant
    in keeping your statutes.
⁶ If I concentrate on your every commandment,
    I can never be put to shame.
⁷ I thank you from an upright heart,
    schooled in your rules of righteousness.
⁸ I mean to observe your statutes;
    never abandon me.

⁹ *Beth* How can a youth remain pure?
    By behaving as your word prescribes.
¹⁰ I have sought you with all my heart,
    do not let me stray from your commandments.
¹¹ I have treasured your promises in my heart,
    since I have no wish to sin against you.
¹² How blessed are you, Yahweh!
    Teach me your statutes!

13 With my lips I have repeated them,
    all these rulings from your own mouth.
14 In the way of your decrees lies my joy,
    a joy beyond all wealth.
15 I mean to meditate on your precepts
    and to concentrate on your paths.
16 I find my delight in your statutes,
    I do not forget your word.

17 *Ghimel* Be good to your servant and I shall live,[b]
    I shall observe your word.
18 Open my eyes: I shall concentrate
    on the marvels of your Law.
19 Exile though I am on earth,
    do not hide your commandments from me.
20 My soul is overcome
    with an incessant longing for your rulings.
21 You reprove the arrogant,[c] the accursed
    who stray from your commandments.
22 Avert[d] their insults and contempt from me,
    since I respect your decrees.
23 Though princes put me on trial,
    your servant will meditate on your statutes,
24 since your decrees are my delight,
    your statutes[e] are my counselors.

25 *Daleth* Down in the dust I lie prostrate:
    revive me as your word has guaranteed.
26 I admitted my behavior, you answered me,
    now teach me your statutes.
27 Explain to me how to keep your precepts,
    that I may meditate on your marvels.
28 I am sleepless with grief:
    raise me as your word has guaranteed.
29 Turn me from the path of delusion,
    grant me the grace of your Law.
30 I have chosen the way of fidelity,
    I have set my heart[f] on your rulings.

31 I cling to your decrees:
   Yahweh, do not disappoint me.
32 I run the way of your commandments,
   since you have set me free.

33 *He* Expound to me the way of your statutes, Yahweh,
   and I will always respect them.[g]
34 Explain[h] to me how to respect your Law
   and how to observe it wholeheartedly.
35 Guide me in the path of your commandments,
   since my delight is there.
36 Turn my heart to your decrees
   and away from getting money.
37 Avert my eyes from lingering on inanities,
   give me life by your word.[i]
38 Keep your promise to your servant,
   so that others in turn may fear you.
39 Avert the insults that I fear,
   in the kindness of your rulings.
40 Look how I yearn for your precepts:
   give me life by your righteousness.

41 *Wau* For, Yahweh, visited by your love
   and saving help, as you have promised,
42 I can find an answer to the insults,
   since I rely on your word.
43 Do not deprive me of that faithful word,
   since my hope has always lain in your rulings.
44 Let me observe your Law unfailingly
   for ever and ever.
45 So, having sought your precepts,
   I shall walk in all freedom.
46 I shall proclaim your decrees to kings
   without fear of disgrace.
47 Your commandments fill me with delight,
   I love them deeply.
48 I stretch out my hands[j] to your beloved commandments,
   I meditate on your statutes.

49 *Zain* Remember the word you pledged your servant,
   on which you have built my hope.
50 This has been my comfort in my suffering:
   that your promise gives me life.
51 Endlessly the arrogant have jeered at me,
   but I have not swerved from your Law.
52 Remembering your rulings in the past,
   Yahweh, I take comfort.
53 Fury grips me when I see the wicked
   abandoning your Law.
54 Where I live in exile,
   your statutes are psalms for me.
55 All night, Yahweh, I remember your name
   and observe your Law.
56 Surely it will count to my credit:
   that I respect your precepts.

57 *Heth* Have I not said, Yahweh, that my task
   is to observe your words?
58 Wholeheartedly I now entreat you,
   take pity on me as you have promised!
59 After reflecting on my behavior,
   I turn my feet to your decrees.
60 Wasting no time, I hurry
   to observe your commandments.
61 Though the nooses of the wicked tighten round me,
   I do not forget your Law.
62 I get up at midnight to thank you
   for the righteousness of your rulings.
63 I am a friend to all who fear you
   and observe your precepts.
64 Yahweh, your love fills the earth:
   teach me your statutes.

65 *Teth* In accordance with your word, Yahweh,
   you have been good to your servant.
66 Teach me good sense and knowledge,
   for I rely on your commandments.

67 In earlier days I had to suffer, I used to stray,
       but now I remember your promise.
68 You, so good and kind,
       teach me your statutes!
69 Though the arrogant tell foul lies about me,
       I wholeheartedly respect your precepts.
70 Their hearts are gross as fat,
       but my delight is in your Law.
71 It was good for me to have to suffer,
       the better to learn your statutes.
72 I put the Law you have given
       before all the gold and silver in the world.

73 *Yod* Yahweh, my maker, my preserver,
       explain your commandments for me to learn.
74 Seeing me, those who fear you will be glad,
       since I put my hope in your word.
75 I know that your rulings are righteous, Yahweh,
       that you make me suffer out of faithfulness.
76 Now, please let your love comfort me,
       as you have promised your servant.
77 Treat me tenderly, and I shall live,
       since your Law is my delight.
78 Shame seize the arrogant who defame me,
       when I meditate on your precepts!
79 May those who fear you rally to me,
       all those familiar with your decrees!
80 Blameless in your statutes be my heart:
       no such shame therefore for me!

81 *Kaph* Keeping my hope in your word,
       I have worn myself out waiting for you to save me,
82 and have strained my eyes waiting for your promise:
       when, I want to know, will you console me?
83 Though smoked as dry as a wineskin,[k]
       I do not forget your statutes.
84 How much longer has your servant to live,
       when will you condemn my persecutors?

85 The arrogant have dug pitfalls for me
  in defiance of your Law.
86 Your commandments epitomize faithfulness;
  when liars hound me, you must help me.
87 Though these wretches have almost done for me,
  I have never abandoned your precepts.
88 Lovingly intervene, give me life,
  and I will observe your decrees.

89 *Lamed* Lasting to eternity, your word,
  Yahweh, unchanging in the heavens:
90 your faithfulness lasts age after age;
  you founded the earth to endure.
91 Creation is maintained by your rulings,
  since all things are your servants.
92 Had your Law not been my delight
  I should have perished in my suffering.
93 I shall never forget your precepts;
  by these you have kept me alive.
94 I am yours, save me,
  since I study your precepts.
95 The wicked may hope to destroy me,
  but I am scrupulous about your decrees.
96 I have noticed limitations to all perfection,
  but your commandment has no limits at all.

97 *Mem* Meditating all day on your Law,
  how I have come to love it!
98 By your commandment, ever mine,
  how much wiser you have made me than my enemies!
99 How much subtler than my teachers,
  through my meditating on your decrees!
100 How much more perceptive than the elders,
  as a result of my respecting your precepts!
101 I refrain my feet from every evil path,
  the better to observe your word.
102 I do not turn aside from your rulings,
  since you yourself teach me these.

103 Your promise, how sweet to my palate!
    Sweeter than honey to my mouth!
104 Your precepts endow me with perception;
    I hate all deceptive paths.

105 *Nun* Now your word is a lamp to my feet,
    a light on my path.
106 I have sworn to observe, I shall maintain,
    your righteous rulings.
107 Yahweh, though my suffering is acute,
    revive me as your word has guaranteed.
108 Yahweh, accept the homage that I offer,
    teach me your rulings.
109 I would lay down my life at any moment,[l]
    I have never yet forgotten your Law.
110 The wicked have tried to trap me,
    but I have never yet veered from your precepts.
111 Your decrees are my eternal heritage,
    they are the joy of my heart.
112 I devote myself to obeying your statutes—
    compensation enough for ever!

113 *Samek* Odious, those whose allegiance is divided;
    I love your Law!
114 You, my refuge and shield,
    I put my hope in your word.
115 Away from me, you wicked people!
    I will respect the commandments of my God.
116 Support me as you have promised, and I shall live,
    do not disappoint me of my hope.
117 Uphold me, and I shall be safe
    with your statutes constantly before my eyes.[m]
118 You spurn all who stray from your statutes,
    their notions being delusion.
119 You scour the wicked off the earth like rust;
    that is why I love your decrees.
120 My whole being trembles before you,
    your rulings fill me with fear.

121 *Ain* Persevering in justice and virtue,
    must I now be abandoned to my oppressors?

122 Guarantor of your servant's well-being,
    forbid the arrogant to oppress me!

123 My eyes are worn out looking for your saving help,
    for your promise of righteousness to come.

124 Treat your servant lovingly,
    teach me your statutes.

125 I am your servant; if you will explain,
    I shall embrace your decrees.

126 Yahweh,[n] now is the time to act,
    your Law is being broken.

127 Yes, I love your commandments
    more than gold, than purest gold.

128 Yes, I rule myself[o] by all your precepts;
    I hate all deceptive paths.

129 *Pe* Your decrees are so wonderful
    my soul cannot but respect them.

130 As your word unfolds, it gives light,
    and the simple understand.

131 I open my mouth, panting
    eagerly for your commandments.

132 Turn to me please, pity me,
    as you should those who love your name.

133 Direct my steps as you have promised,[p]
    let evil win no power over me.

134 Rescue me from human oppression;
    I will observe your precepts.

135 Treat your servant kindly,
    teach me your statutes.

136 My eyes stream with tears,
    because others disregard your Law.

137 *Sade* Righteous, indeed, Yahweh!
    And all your rulings correct!

138 The decrees you impose, how righteous,
    how absolutely faithful!

139 Zeal for your house^q devours me,
     since my oppressors forget your word.
140 But your promise is well tested,
     and your servant holds it dear.
141 Puny and despised as I am,
     I do not forget your precepts.
142 Your righteousness is eternal righteousness,
     your Law holds true for ever.
143 Though distress and anguish grip me,
     your commandments are my delight.
144 Eternally righteous, your decrees—
     explain them to me, and I shall live.

145 *Qoph* Sincere, my call—Yahweh, answer me!
     I will respect your statutes.
146 I invoke you, save me,
     I will observe your decrees.
147 I am up before dawn to call for help,
     I put my hope in your word.
148 I lie awake throughout the night,
     to meditate on your promise.
149 In your love, Yahweh, listen to my voice,
     let your rulings give me life.
150 My cruel persecutors^r are closing in,
     how remote they are from your Law!
151 But, Yahweh, you are closer still
     and all your commandments are true.
152 Long have I known that your decrees
     were founded to last for ever.

153 *Resh* Take note of my suffering and rescue me,
     for I do not forget your Law.
154 Take up my cause, defend me,^s
     give me life as you have promised.
155 You will never save the wicked,
     if they do not study your statutes,
156 but many are your mercies to me, Yahweh,
     by your rulings give me life.

157 Many hound me and oppress me,
       but I do not swerve from your decrees.
158 The sight of these renegades disgusts me,
       they do not observe your promise;
159 but, Yahweh, see how I love your precepts,
       and lovingly give me life.
160 Faithfulness is the essence[t] of your word,
       your righteous rulings hold good for ever.

161 *Shin* Unjustifiably though princes hound me,
       your word is what fills me with dread.
162 I rejoice in your promise,
       like someone on finding a vast treasure.
163 I hate, I detest, delusion;
       your Law is what I love.
164 Seven times daily I praise you
       for your righteous rulings.
165 Universal peace for those who love your Law,
       no stumbling blocks for them!
166 Waiting for you, Yahweh, my savior,
       I fulfill your commandments.
167 My soul observes your decrees;
       these I wholly love.
168 I observe your precepts, your decrees;
       you know how I keep to your paths.

169 *Tau* Yahweh, may my cry approach your presence;
       let your word endow me with perception!
170 May my entreaty reach your presence;
       rescue me as you have promised.
171 May my lips proclaim your praise,
       since you teach me your statutes.
172 May my tongue recite your promise,
       since all your commandments are righteous.
173 May your hand be there to help me,
       since I have chosen your precepts.
174 I long for you, Yahweh, my savior,
       your Law is my delight.

175 Long may my soul live to praise you,
      long be your rulings my help!
176 I am wandering like a lost sheep:[u]
      come and look for your servant.

No, I have never forgotten your commandments.

PSALM 120   V 119

The enemies of peace

Song of Ascents[a]

1 When I am in trouble, I call to
   Yahweh, and he answers me.
2 Yahweh, save me from these lying lips
   and these faithless tongues!

3 How will he pay back the false oath[b]
   of a faithless tongue?
4 With war arrows hardened
   over red-hot charcoal!

5 This is worse than a life in Meshech,[c]
   or camping in Kedar!

6 Too long have I lived
   among people who hate peace,
7 who, when I propose peace,[d]
   are all for war.

PSALM 121

The guardian of Israel[a]

Song of Ascents

1 I lift my eyes to the mountains:
   where is help to come from?
2 Help comes to me from Yahweh,
   who made heaven and earth.

3 No letting our footsteps slip!
   This guard of yours, he does not doze!
4 The guardian of Israel
   does not doze or sleep.

5 Yahweh guards you, shades you.
   With Yahweh at your right hand
6 sun cannot strike you down by day,
   nor moon at night.

7 Yahweh guards you from harm,
   he guards your lives,
8 he guards you leaving, coming back,
   now and for always.

PSALM 122

Hail, Jerusalem!*a*

Song of Ascents – Of David

1 How I rejoiced when they said to me,
   "Let us go to the house of Yahweh!"
2 And now our feet are standing
   in your gateways, Jerusalem.

3 Jerusalem restored! The city,
   one united whole!*b*
4 Here the tribes come up,
   the tribes of Yahweh,

   they come to praise Yahweh's name,
   as he ordered Israel,
5 here where the tribunals of justice are,
   the royal tribunals of David.

6 Pray for peace in Jerusalem,
   "Prosperity to your houses!*c*
7 Peace inside your city walls!
   Prosperity to your palaces!"

8 Since all are my brothers and friends,
   I say, "Peace be with you!"
9 Since Yahweh our God lives here,
   I pray for your happiness.

Prayer of the distressed[a]

Song of Ascents

1 I lift my eyes to you,
    to you who have your home in heaven,
2 eyes like the eyes of slaves
    fixed on their master's hand;

  like the eyes of a slave girl
    fixed on the hand of her mistress,
  so our eyes are fixed on Yahweh our God,
    for him to take pity on us;

3 pity us, Yahweh, take pity on us,
    we have had more than our share of scorn,
4 more than our share
    of jeers from the complacent,
    of scorn from the proud.[b]

PSALM 124   V 123

The savior of Israel[a]

Song of Ascents—Of David

1 If Yahweh had not been on our side
    —let Israel repeat it—
2 if Yahweh had not been on our side
    when they attacked us,

3 they would have swallowed us alive
   and burnt us to death in their rage.

4 The waters would have closed over us,
   the torrent have swept us away,
5 either would have drowned us
   in their turbulent waves.

6 Blessed be Yahweh who did not let us fall
   a victim to those teeth,
7 who let us escape like birds
   from the fowler's net.

He tore the net
and we escaped;
8 our help is in the name of Yahweh,
   who made heaven and earth.

PSALM 125   V 124

God protects his faithful

Song of Ascents

1 Those who trust in Yahweh are like Mount Zion,
   unshakable, standing for ever.
2 Jerusalem! Encircled by mountains,
   as Yahweh encircles his people
   now and for always.

3 No wicked scepter shall rule[a]
   this heritage of the virtuous,
   or the virtuous in their turn
   might take to evil.

4 Yahweh, be good to the good,
   to those of upright heart.

⁵ But the perverts, those who follow twisting paths—
    may Yahweh send them to join the evildoers!

Peace to Israel!

PSALM 126
Song of the returning exiles^a

Song of Ascents

¹ When Yahweh brought Zion's captives home,
    at first it seemed like a dream;
² then our mouths filled with laughter
    and our lips with song.

Even the pagans started talking
    about the marvels Yahweh had done for us!
³ What marvels indeed he did for us,
    and how overjoyed we were!

⁴ Yahweh, bring all our captives back again
    like torrents in the Negeb!^b
⁵ Those who went sowing in tears
    now sing as they reap.

⁶ They went away, went away weeping,
    carrying the seed;
they come back, come back singing,
    carrying their sheaves.

PSALM 127

Trust in Providence[a]

Song of Ascents – Of Solomon

1 If Yahweh does not build the house,
    in vain the masons toil;
  if Yahweh does not guard the city,
    in vain the sentries watch.

2 In vain you get up earlier,
    and put off going to bed,
  sweating to make a living,
    since he provides for his beloved as they sleep.[b]

3 Sons are a bounty from Yahweh,
    he rewards with descendants:
4 like the arrows in a hero's hand
    are the sons you father when young.

5 Happy the man who has filled his quiver
    with arrows of this sort;
  in dispute with his enemies at the gate,[c]
    he will not be worsted.

PSALM 128

V 127

Blessing for the devout[a]

Song of Ascents

1 Happy, all those who fear Yahweh
    and follow in his paths.

205

2 You will eat what your hands have worked for,
    happiness and prosperity will be yours.
3 Your wife: a fruitful vine
    on the inner walls of your house.
  Your sons: round your table
    like shoots round an olive tree.

4 Such are the blessings that fall
    on the man who fears Yahweh.
5a May Yahweh bless you from Zion
5c all the days of your life!
5b May you see Jerusalem prosperous
6 and live to see your children's children!

    Peace to Israel!

PSALM 129   V 128

Against the enemies of Zion

Song of Ascents

1 Hard as they have harried me since I was young[a]
    —let Israel repeat it—
2 hard as they have harried me since I was young,
    they have not overcome me.
3 Plowmen have plowed on my back
    longer and longer furrows,
4 but now Yahweh the Righteous has shattered
    the yoke of the wicked.

5 May they all be thrown into confusion, be routed,
    who have hated Zion,
6 be blasted by winds from the east like grass[b]
    sprouting on the roof!

7 Roof grass never yet filled
      reaper's arm or binder's lap—
8 and no one passing them will ever say,
      "Yahweh's blessing on you!"

We bless you in the name of Yahweh.

PSALM 130

From the depths[a]

Song of Ascents

1 From the depths I call to you, Yahweh,
2 Lord, listen to my cry for help!
   Listen compassionately
      to my pleading!

3 If you never overlooked our sins, Yahweh,
   Lord, could anyone survive?
4 But you do forgive us:
      and for that we revere you.[b]

5 [c]I wait for Yahweh, my soul waits for him,
      I rely on his promise,
6   my soul relies on the Lord
      more than a watchman on the coming of dawn.

7 Let Israel rely on Yahweh
      as much as the watchman on the dawn!
   For it is with Yahweh that mercy is to be found,
   and a generous redemption;
8 it is he who redeems Israel
      from all their sins.

Childlike trust in God[a]

Song of Ascents – Of David

¹ Yahweh, my heart has no lofty ambitions,
   my eyes do not look too high.
  I am not concerned with great affairs
   or marvels beyond my scope.
² Enough for me to keep my soul tranquil and quiet
   like a child in its mother's arms,
  as content as a child that has been weaned.

³ Israel, rely on Yahweh,
   now and for always!

PSALM 132   V 131

The ark is taken to Zion: anniversary hymn[a]

Song of Ascents

¹ Yahweh, remember David
   and all the hardships he suffered,
² and the oath he swore to Yahweh,
   his vow to the Mighty One of Jacob:

³ not to enter tent or house,
   not to climb into bed,
⁴ not to allow himself to sleep,
   not even to close his eyes,

⁵ until he had found a place for Yahweh,
a home for the Mighty One of Jacob!

⁶ Listen: we heard it*ᵇ* was in Ephrathah,
we found it at Fields-of-the-Forest!*ᶜ*
⁷ Let us go where he*ᵈ* is waiting
and worship at his footstool.

⁸ Yahweh, go up to your resting place,
you and your ark of power.
⁹ Your priests are vesting in virtue
and your devout are shouting for joy.
¹⁰ For the sake of your servant David,
do not banish your anointed.

¹¹ Yahweh swore to David
and will remain true to his word,
"I promise that your own son
shall succeed you on the throne.

¹² "If your sons observe my covenant,
the decrees that I have taught them,
their sons too shall succeed you
on the throne for evermore."

¹³ For Yahweh has chosen Zion,
desiring this to be his home,
¹⁴ "Here I will stay for ever,
this is the home I have chosen.

¹⁵ "I will bless her virtuous*ᵉ* with riches,
provide her poor with food,
¹⁶ vest her priests in salvation
and her devout shall shout for joy.

¹⁷ "Here, I will make a horn sprout for David,
here, I will trim a lamp*ᶠ* for my anointed,
¹⁸ whose enemies I shall clothe in shame,
while his*ᵍ* crown bursts into flower."

Brotherly love[a]

Song of Ascents – Of David

1 How good, how delightful it is
  for all to live together like brothers:

2 fine as oil on the head,
   running down the beard,
  running down Aaron's beard[b]
   to the collar of his robes;

3 copious as a Hermon dew
   falling on the heights of Zion,
  where Yahweh confers his blessing,
   everlasting life.

PSALM 134   V 133

Night hymn[a]

Song of Ascents

1 Come, bless Yahweh,
  all you who serve Yahweh,
  serving in the house of Yahweh,
  in the courts of the house of our God![b]

2 Stretch out your hands toward the sanctuary,
  bless Yahweh night after night!

3 May Yahweh bless you from Zion,
  he who made heaven and earth![c]

PSALM 135

Hymn of praise[a]

1 Alleluia!

Praise the name of Yahweh,
praise Yahweh, you who serve him,
2 serving in the house of Yahweh,
in the courts of the house of our God!

3 Praise Yahweh, for Yahweh is good.
Play for his name, for he inspires love;
4 since Yahweh has chosen Jacob,
Israel as his own.

5 I have learnt for myself that Yahweh is great,
that our Lord surpasses all other gods.
6 In the heavens, on the earth,
in the ocean, in the depths,
Yahweh's will is sovereign.

7 He raises up clouds from the boundaries of earth,
makes the lightning flash for the downpour
and brings the wind out of his storehouse.

8 He struck down the firstborn of Egypt,
of man and beast alike,
9 he sent signs and wonders
among you, Egypt,
against Pharaoh and his officials.

10 He struck the pagans down in droves,
he slaughtered mighty kings,
11 Sihon, king of the Amorites,
and Og, the king of Bashan,
and all the kingdoms of Canaan;
12 he gave their lands as a legacy,
a legacy to his people Israel.

¹³ Yahweh, your name endures for ever!
Yahweh, your memory is always fresh!
¹⁴ Since Yahweh vindicates his people,
and cares for those who serve him;

¹⁵ whereas pagans' idols, in silver and gold,
products of human skill,
¹⁶ have mouths, but never speak,
eyes, but never see,

¹⁷ ears, but never hear,
and not a breath in their mouths.
¹⁸ Their makers will end up like them
and so will anyone who relies on them.

¹⁹ House of Israel, bless Yahweh,
House of Aaron, bless Yahweh,
²⁰ House of Levi, bless Yahweh,
you who fear Yahweh, bless Yahweh!

²¹ Blessed be Yahweh in Zion,
in Jerusalem his home!

PSALM 136   V 135

Litany of thanksgiving[a]

Alleluia![b]

¹ Give thanks to Yahweh, for he is good,
his love is everlasting!
² Give thanks to the God of gods,
his love is everlasting!
³ Give thanks to the Lord of lords,
his love is everlasting!

⁴ He alone performs great marvels,
his love is everlasting!

5 His wisdom made the heavens,
   his love is everlasting!
6 He set the earth on the waters,
   his love is everlasting!

7 He made the great lights,
   his love is everlasting!
8 The sun to govern the day,
   his love is everlasting!
9 Moon and stars to govern the night,
   his love is everlasting!

10 He struck down the firstborn of Egypt,
   his love is everlasting!
11 And brought Israel out,
   his love is everlasting!
12 With mighty hand and outstretched arm,
   his love is everlasting!

13 He split the Sea of Reeds,
   his love is everlasting!
14 Led Israel through the middle,
   his love is everlasting!
15 Drowned Pharaoh and his army,
   his love is everlasting!

16 He led his people through the wilderness,
   his love is everlasting!
17 He struck down mighty kings,
   his love is everlasting!

18 He slaughtered famous kings,
   his love is everlasting!
19 Sihon, king of the Amorites,
   his love is everlasting!
20 And Og, the king of Bashan,
   his love is everlasting!

21 He gave their lands as a legacy,
   his love is everlasting!

22 A legacy to his servant Israel,
    his love is everlasting!
23 He remembered us when we were down,
    his love is everlasting!
24 And snatched us from our oppressors,
    his love is everlasting!
25 He provides for all living creatures,
    his love is everlasting!
26 Give thanks to the God of Heaven,
    his love is everlasting!

PSALM 137

Ballad of the exiles[a]

1 Beside the streams of Babylon
    we sat and wept
    at the memory of Zion,
2 leaving our harps
    hanging on the poplars there.

3 For we had been asked
    to sing to our captors,
    to entertain those who had carried us off:[b]
    "Sing," they said,
    "some hymns of Zion."

4 How could we sing
    one of Yahweh's hymns
    in a pagan country?
5 Jerusalem, if I forget you,
    may my right hand wither![c]

6 May I never speak again,
    if I forget you!
    If I do not count Jerusalem
    the greatest of my joys!

214

7 Yahweh, remember
what the Sons of Edom did
on the day of Jerusalem,[d]
how they said, "Down with her!
Raze her to the ground!"

8 Destructive[e] Daughter of Babel,
a blessing on the man who treats you
as you have treated us,
9 a blessing on him who takes and dashes
your babies against the rock!

PSALM 138   V 137

Hymn of thanksgiving

Of David

1 I thank you, Yahweh, with all my heart,
because you have heard what I said.[a]
In the presence of the angels[b] I play for you,
2 and bow down toward your holy Temple.

I give thanks to your name for your love and faithfulness;
your promise is even greater than your fame.[c]
3 The day I called for help, you heard me
and you increased my strength.[d]

4 Yahweh, all kings on earth give thanks to you,
for they have heard your promises;
5 they celebrate Yahweh's actions,
"Great is the glory of Yahweh!"
6 From far above, Yahweh sees the humble,
from far away he marks down the arrogant.

⁷ Though I live surrounded by trouble,
you keep me alive—to my enemies' fury!
You stretch your hand out and save me,
⁸ your right hand will do everything for me.^e
Yahweh, your love is everlasting,
do not abandon us whom you have made.

PSALM 139

In praise of God's omniscience^a

For the choirmaster – Of David – Psalm

¹ Yahweh, you examine me and know me,
² you know if I am standing or sitting,
you read my thoughts from far away,
³ whether I walk or lie down, you are watching,
you know every detail of my conduct.

⁴ The word is not even on my tongue,
Yahweh, before you know all about it;
⁵ close behind and close in front you fence me round,
shielding me with your hand.
⁶ Such knowledge is beyond my understanding,
a height to which my mind cannot attain.

⁷ Where could I go to escape your spirit?
Where could I flee from your presence?
⁸ If I climb the heavens, you are there,
there too, if I lie in Sheol.

⁹ If I flew to the point of sunrise,
or westward across the sea,
¹⁰ your hand would still be guiding me,
your right hand holding me.

11 If I asked darkness to cover me,[b]
   and light to become night around me,
12 that darkness would not be dark to you,
   night would be as light as day.[c]

13 It was you who created my inmost self,
   and put me together in my mother's womb;
14 for all these mysteries I thank you:
   for the wonder of myself, for the wonder of your works.[d]

   You know me[e] through and through,
15 from having watched my bones take shape
   when I was being formed in secret,
   knitted together in the limbo of the womb.[f]

16 You had scrutinized my every action,[g]
   all were recorded in your book,[h]
   my days[i] listed and determined,
17 even before the first of them occurred.[j]

   God, how hard it is to grasp your thoughts!
   How impossible to count them!
18 I could no more count them than I could the sand,
   and suppose I could,[k] you would still be with me.[l]

19 God, if only you would kill the wicked!
   Men of blood, away from me!
20 They talk blasphemously about you,
   regard your thoughts as nothing.

21 Yahweh, do I not hate those who hate you,
   and loathe those who defy you?
22 I hate them with a total hatred,
   I regard them as my own enemies.

23 God, examine me and know my heart,
   probe me and know my thoughts;
24 make sure I do not follow pernicious ways,
   and guide me in the way that is everlasting.

PSALM 140

Against the wicked

For the choirmaster – Psalm – Of David

1 Yahweh, rescue me from evil people,
    defend me from men of violence,
2 from people plotting evil,
    forever intent on stirring up strife,
3 who make their tongues as sharp as serpents'
    with vipers' venom on their lips.   *Pause*

4 Yahweh, guard me from attacks by the wicked,
    defend me from those who love force,
  from people plotting to make me stumble,
5b   forever laying snares where I walk,[a]
5a insolent wretches, concealing pitfall and noose
5c   to trap me as I pass.   *Pause*

6 I have told Yahweh, "You are my God."
    Yahweh, listen to my cry for help.
7 Yahweh, my Lord, my saving strength,
    shielding my head when I have to fight,
8 Yahweh, do not grant their wicked wishes,
    do not let their plots succeed.

9 May those besieging me not win,[b]   *Pause*
    may their own cruel words overtake them,
10 may red-hot embers rain down on them,[c]
    may they be flung into the abyss for good,
11 may evil hound the man of violence to death
    and the slanderer[d] not hold his own on earth.

218

¹² I know Yahweh will avenge the wretched,
    and see justice done for the poor.
¹³ The virtuous shall have good cause to thank your name,
    and the upright to find a home with you.

PSALM 141   V *140*

Against the attractions of evil

Psalm – Of David

¹ Yahweh, I am calling, hurry to me,
    listen to me, I am invoking you.
² My prayers rise like incense,
    my hands like the evening offering.^{*a*}

³ Yahweh, set a guard at my mouth,
    a watcher at the gate of my lips.
⁴ Let me feel no impulse to do wrong,
    to share the godlessness of evildoers.

No, I will not sample their delights.
⁵ A virtuous man may strike me in reproof, for my own
    good,
    but a wicked one shall never anoint my head with oil!^{*b*}
    Daily I counter their malice with prayer.^{*c*}
⁶ When their judges are flung on jagged rock,^{*d*}
    they will learn how mild my words have been,
⁷ "Like a millstone smashed^{*e*} on the ground,
    our bones are scattered at the mouth of Sheol."

⁸ To you, Yahweh my Lord, I turn my eyes.
    I take shelter in you, do not leave me exposed!
⁹ Keep me out of traps that are set for me,
    from the bait laid for me by evil men.
¹⁰ Let the wicked fall into their^{*f*} own net,
    while I go on my way.

Prayer of a hunted man[a]

Poem – Of David – When he was in the cave – Psalm

1 To Yahweh, my cry! I plead.
  To Yahweh, my cry! I entreat.
2 I pour out my supplications,
  I unfold all my troubles;
3 my spirit fails me,
  but you, you know my path.

On the path I follow
they have concealed a trap.
4 Look on my right[b] and see,
  there is no one to befriend me.
  All help is denied me,
  no one cares about me.

5 I invoke you, Yahweh,
  I affirm that you are my refuge,
  my heritage in the land of the living.[c]
6 Listen to my cries for help,
  I can hardly be crushed lower.

Rescue me from persecutors
stronger than I am!
7 Free me from this imprisonment,
  and I will thank your name once more
  in the Assembly of the virtuous,[d]
  for the goodness you show me.

A humble entreaty

Psalm – Of David

1 Yahweh, hear my prayer,
   listen to my pleading,
   answer me faithfully, righteously;
2 do not put your servant on trial,
   no one is virtuous by your standards.[a]

3 An enemy who hounds me
   to crush me into the dust,
   forces me to dwell in darkness
   like the dead of long ago;
4 my spirit fails me
   and my heart is full of fear.

5 I recall the days of old,
   I reflect on all that you did,
   I ponder your deeds;
6 I stretch out my hands,
   like thirsty ground I yearn for you.   *Pause*

7 Quick, Yahweh, answer me
   before my spirit fails;
   if you hide your face much longer,
   I shall go down to the Pit like the rest.

8 Let dawn bring proof of your love,
   for one who relies on you;
   let it show the right road,
   to one who lifts up his soul to you.

[9] Yahweh, rescue me from my enemies,
I have fled[b] to you for shelter;
[10] teach me to obey you,
since you are my God;
may your good spirit guide me
on to level ground.

[11] Yahweh, for the sake of your name,
keep your promise to save me;
protect me from oppression,
[12] love me, kill my enemies,
destroy my oppressors,
for I am your servant.

PSALM 144 V *143*

War hymn and the fruits of victory[a]

Of David

[1] Blessed be Yahweh, my rock,
who trains my hands for war
and my fingers for battle,
[2] my love, my bastion,
my citadel, my savior,
I shelter behind him, my shield,
he makes the nations submit to me.

[3] Yahweh, what is man, that you should notice him?
A human being, that you should think about him?
[4] Man's life, a mere puff of wind,
his days, as fugitive as shadows.

[5] Yahweh, lower your heavens, come down to us!
Touch the mountains, make them smoke,
[6] flash your lightning—scatter them,
shoot your arrows—rout them.

7 Reach down your hand from above,
   save me, rescue me from deep waters,
   from the power of aliens
8 who tell nothing but lies,
   who are prepared to swear to falsehood!

9 God, I have made a new song for you
   to be played on the ten-string lyre,
10 you who give victory to kings
   and safety to your servant David.[b]

11 From peril of sword save me,
   rescue me from the power of aliens
   who tell nothing but lies,
   who are prepared to swear to falsehood!

12 May our sons be like plants
      growing strong from their earliest days,
   our daughters like corner-statues,[c]
      carvings fit for a palace;
13 may our barns overflow
      with every possible crop,
   may the sheep in our fields be counted
      in their thousands and tens of thousands,

14 may our cattle be stout and strong;
      and may there be an end of raids and exile,
   and of panic in our streets.

15 Happy the nation of whom this is true,
   happy the nation whose God is Yahweh!

Hymn of praise to Yahweh the king

Hymn – Of David

1 *Aleph* I sing your praises, God my King,
   I bless your name for ever and ever,
2 *Beth* blessing you day after day,
   and praising your name for ever and ever.
3 *Ghimel* Can anyone measure the magnificence
   of Yahweh the great, and his inexpressible grandeur?

4 *Daleth* Celebrating your acts of power,
   one age shall praise your doings to another.
5 *He* Oh, the splendor of your glory, your renown![a]
   I tell myself the story of your marvelous deeds.[b]
6 *Wau* Men will proclaim your fearful power
   and I shall assert your greatness;
7 *Zain* they will celebrate your generous kindness
   and joyfully acclaim your righteousness.

8 *Heth* He, Yahweh, is merciful, tenderhearted,
   slow to anger, very loving,
9 *Teth* and universally kind; Yahweh's tenderness
   embraces all his creatures.

10 *Yod* Yahweh, all your creatures thank you,
   and your faithful bless you.
11 *Kaph* Kingly and glorious they proclaim you,
   they affirm your might.

12 *Lamed* Let mankind learn your acts of power,
   and the majestic glory of your sovereignty!
13 *Mem* Your sovereignty is an eternal sovereignty,
   your empire lasts from age to age.

(*Nun*) Always true to his promises,
Yahweh shows love in all he does.[c]

14 *Samek* Only stumble, and Yahweh at once supports you,
if others bow you down, he will raise you up.

15 *Ain* Patiently all creatures look to you
to feed them throughout the year;
16 *Pe* quick to satisfy every need,
you[d] feed them all with a generous hand.

17 *Sade* Righteous in all that he does,
Yahweh acts only out of love,
18 *Qoph* standing close to all who invoke him,
close to all who invoke Yahweh faithfully.

19 *Resh* Those who fear him need only to ask to be answered;
he hears their cries for help and saves them.
20 *Shin* Under his protection the pious are safe,
but Yahweh is destruction to the wicked.

21 *Tau* Yahweh's praise be ever in my mouth,
and let every creature bless his holy name
for ever and ever!

PSALM 146   V *145*

Hymn to the God of help[a]

1 Alleluia!

Praise Yahweh, my soul!
2 I mean to praise Yahweh all my life,
I mean to sing to my God as long as I live.

³ Do not put your trust in men in power,
or in any mortal man—he cannot save,
⁴ he yields his breath and goes back to the earth he came
from,
and on that day all his schemes perish.

⁵ Happy the man who has the God of Jacob to help him
whose hope is fixed on Yahweh his God,
⁶ maker of heaven and earth,
and the sea, and all that these hold!

Yahweh, forever faithful,
⁷ gives justice to those denied it,
gives food to the hungry,
gives liberty to prisoners.

⁸ᵃ Yahweh restores sight to the blind,
⁸ᵇ Yahweh straightens the bent,
⁹ᵃ Yahweh protects the stranger,
⁹ᵇ he keeps the orphan and widow.

⁸ᶜ Yahweh loves the virtuous,
⁹ᶜ and frustrates the wicked.
¹⁰ Yahweh reigns for ever,
your God, Zion, from age to age.

PSALM 147   V 146–147

Hymn to the Almighty[a]

Alleluia![b]
¹ Praise Yahweh—it is good to sing
in honor of our God—sweet is his praise.[c]

² Yahweh, Restorer of Jerusalem!
He brought back Israel's exiles,
³ healing their broken hearts,
and binding up their wounds.

4   He decides the number of the stars
    and gives each of them a name;
5   our Lord is great, all-powerful,
    of infinite understanding.

6   Yahweh, who lifts up the humble,
    humbles the wicked to the ground.

7   Sing to Yahweh in gratitude,
    play the lyre for our God:

8   who covers the heavens with clouds,
    to provide the earth with rain,
    to produce fresh grass on the hillsides
    and the plants that are needed by man,[d]
9   who gives their food to the cattle
    and to the young ravens when they cry.

10   The strength of the war horse means nothing to him,
    it is not infantry that interests him.
11   Yahweh is interested only in those who fear him,
    in those who rely on his love.

12   Praise Yahweh, Jerusalem,
    Zion, praise your God:[e]
13   for strengthening the bars of your gates,
    for blessing your citizens,
14   for granting you peace on your frontiers,
    for feeding you on the finest wheat.

15   He gives an order;
    his word flashes to earth:[f]
16   to spread snow like a blanket,
    to strew hoarfrost like ashes,

17   to drop ice like bread crumbs,
    and when the cold is unbearable,
18   he sends his word to bring the thaw
    and warm wind to melt the snow.

19 He reveals his word to Jacob,
   his statutes and rulings to Israel:
20 he never does this for other nations,
   he never reveals his rulings to them.

PSALM 148

Cosmic hymn of praise

1 Alleluia!

Let heaven praise Yahweh:
praise him, heavenly heights,
2 praise him, all his angels,
praise him, all his armies!

3 Praise him, sun and moon,
praise him, shining stars,
4 praise him, highest heavens,
and waters above the heavens!

5 Let them all praise the name of Yahweh,[a]
at whose command they were created;
6 he has fixed them in their place for ever,
by an unalterable statute.

7 Let earth praise Yahweh:
sea monsters and all the deeps,
8 fire and hail, snow and mist,
gales that obey his decree,

9 mountains and hills,
orchards and forests,
10 wild animals and farm animals,
snakes and birds,

¹¹ all kings on earth and nations,
princes, all rulers in the world,
¹² young men and girls,
old people, and children too!

¹³ Let them all praise the name of Yahweh,
for his name and no other is sublime,
transcending earth and heaven in majesty,
¹⁴ raising the fortunes of[b] his people,
to the praises of the devout,
of Israel, the people dear to him.

PSALM 149

Song of triumph[a]

¹ Alleluia!

Sing Yahweh a new song,
let the congregation of the faithful sing his praise!
² Let Israel rejoice in his maker,
and Zion's children exult in their King;
³ let them dance in praise of his name,
playing to him on strings and drums!
⁴ For Yahweh has been kind to his people,
conferring victory on us who are weak;
⁵ the faithful exult in triumph,
prostrate before God[b] they acclaim him
⁶ with panegyrics on their lips,
and a two-edged sword in their hands

⁷ to exact vengeance on the pagans,
to inflict punishment on the heathen,
⁸ to shackle their kings with chains
and their nobles with fetters,
⁹ to execute the preordained sentence.[c]
Thus gloriously are the faithful rewarded!

PSALM 150
Final chorus of praise[a]

1 Alleluia!

Praise God in his temple on earth,
praise him in his temple in heaven,
2 praise him for his mighty achievements,
praise him for his transcendent greatness!

3 Praise him with blasts of the trumpet,
praise him with lyre and harp,
4 praise him with drums and dancing,
praise him with strings and reeds,
5 praise him with clashing cymbals,
praise him with clanging cymbals!
6 Let everything that breathes praise Yahweh!

Alleluia!

List of Abbreviations of books of the Bible used in notes in alphabetical order of abbreviations

Ac	. . . . Acts	3 Jn	. . . . 3 John
Am	. . . . Amos	Jon	. . . . Jonah
Ba	. . . Baruch	Jos	. . . Joshua
1 Ch	. . 1 Chronicles	Jr	. . . Jeremiah
2 Ch	. . 2 Chronicles	Jude	. . . . Jude
1 Co	. . 1 Corinthians	1 K	. . . 1 Kings
2 Co	. . 2 Corinthians	2 K	. . . 2 Kings
Col	. . . Colossians	Lk	. . . . Luke
Dn	. . . . Daniel	Lm	. . Lamentations
Dt	. . Deuteronomy	Lv	. . . Leviticus
Ep	. . . Ephesians	1 M	. . 1 Maccabees
Est	. . . . Esther	2 M	. . 2 Maccabees
Ex	. . . . Exodus	Mi	. . . . Micah
Ezk	. . . Ezekiel	Mk	. . . . Mark
Ezr	. . . . Ezra	Ml	. . . Malachi
Ga	. . . Galatians	Mt	. . . Matthew
Gn	. . . Genesis	Na	. . . Nahum
Hab	. . Habakkuk	Nb	. . . Numbers
Heb	. . . Hebrews	Ne	. . . Nehemiah
Hg	. . . . Haggai	Ob	. . . Obadiah
Ho	. . . . Hosea	1 P	. . . 1 Peter
Is	. . . . Isaiah	2 P	. . . 2 Peter
Jb	. . . . . Job	Ph	. . Philippians
Jdt	. . . . Judith	Phm	. . Philemon
Jg	. . . . Judges	Pr	. . . Proverbs
Jl	. . . . . Joel	Ps	. . . Psalms
Jm	. . . . James	Qo	. . Ecclesiastes
Jn	. . . . John	Rm	. . . Romans
1 Jn	. . . 1 John	Rt	. . . . Ruth
2 Jn	. . . 2 John	Rv	. . Revelation

1 S	. . . . 1 Samuel	1 Tm	. . .	1 Timothy
2 S	. . . . 2 Samuel	2 Tm	. . .	2 Timothy
Sg	. . Song of Songs	Tt	. . . .	. Titus
Si	. . Ecclesiasticus	Ws	. . .	. Wisdom
Tb	. . . . . Tobit	Zc	. . .	. Zechariah
1 Th	. . 1 Thessalonians	Zp	. . .	Zephaniah
2 Th	. . 2 Thessalonians			

Other Abbreviations not in common use

Add.	. additional words included by some authorities	Lat.	. . . . Latin
		LXX	. the Greek "Septuagint"
Arab.	. . . . Arabic	M.T.	. Massoretic Text
Ch.	. the "Chronicler" (as well as the Books of Chronicles)	Om.	. words omitted by some authorities
		Sam.	. . Samaritan Pentateuch
Ch.	. . . chapter(s)	Theod.	. . Theodotian
Conj.	. conjectural reading	Var.	. variant reading
		Vet. Lat.	. . . Old Latin version
Corr.	. . text has been corrected		
		Vulg.	. . . Vulgate
Hebr.	. . Hebrew language/text		

232

NOTES

Psalm 1

a. Ps 1 and 2 serve as preface to the Psalter; they summarize its moral teaching and messianic ideas. Ps 1 contrasts "the two ways" to the advantage of the Law, man's true way to happiness. Cf. 19:7–14 and 119.

b. Reading in an undertone, a meditative prayer (63:6; 77:12; 143:5) as opposed to the loud cry of the sufferer (3:4; 5:2; etc.).

c. The great Judgment to come, according to the Massoretic text ("the" Judgment); any divine judgment in this life, according to Greek ("a" judgment).

Psalm 2

a. Jewish and Christian tradition regard this psalm as messianic in the same way as 110 on which it possibly depends. Its horizon is the future messianic age. In the liturgy it is used for feasts of the incarnate Word.

b. The rebels speak, v. 3, then Yahweh himself, v. 6, finally the Messiah, v. 7f. By consecrating him king of Israel, v. 6, God pronounces him "his son"; the phrase in this context is familiar in the ancient East, but in conjunction with the messianic promise of 2 S 7 it will be given a deeper meaning; Heb 1:5, followed by Christian tradition and liturgy, applies v. 7 to the eternal generation of the Word.

c. The messianic King is here portrayed as a warrior, a traditional representation.

d. Corr. Hebr. "and shake with trembling; kiss the Son."

Psalm 3

a. The Fathers apply this passage to the death and resurrection of Christ.

Psalm 4

a. Trust and thanks: God is the one source of happiness. Vv. 4 and 8 show that it is an evening prayer.

b. Versions; "answer me!" Hebr.

c. Lit. "why be dull-hearted" Greek; "my honor is shamed" Hebr.

d. We should shrink from offending God and pray to him in the calm silence of adoration. "spend . . . meditation" lit. "speak in your hearts on your beds and be silent."

e. Biblical phrase, common in the Psalter, for royal or divine favor. Lit. "Lift up the light of your face on us." The Greek and Vulg. translation "The light of your face is sealed (or: signed) on us" has been applied in the baptismal liturgy to the signing with the baptismal "character" which makes the Christian a "child of the light," Lk 16:8; Jn 8:12+; 1 Th 5:5; Ep 5:8.

Psalm 5

a. The morning is regarded as the time of God's favor, 17:15+.

b. Translations vary: I present my request; I offer my prayer; I prepare my sacrifice . . .

c. Lit. "because of my enemies."

d. Such appeals for vengeance on the enemies of God or the psalmist are very frequent, cf. for example 10:15; 31:17; 54:5; 58:6f; 59:11f; 69:22–28; 79:12; 83:9–18; 104:35; 109:6–20; 125:5; 137:7–9; 139:19–22; 140:9–11. Under the Old Covenant retribution in this life was still the rule, and against this background these appeals betray simply a hunger for justice. Personal experience and growing revelation will show the inadequacy of this outlook: the way of God's justice must remain a mystery to man (cf. Jb). The N.T. refines the outlook still further: justice must give way to love, Mt 5:43–48. Thus purged of personal resentment, the psalms of revenge remain, for the Church and the individual Christian, an expression of that same hunger for justice in the face of forces which are ever-present in the world.

Psalm 6

a. First of the seven "Penitential Psalms" (32, 38, 51, 102, 130, 143). A sick man speaks to God.

b. The Hebr. word means life-giving breath (and by extension "throat") which is the source of life and which disappears at death. "My soul" is often used for the reflexive pronoun "myself," as are also "my life," "my glory," "my face."

c. In Sheol, cf. Nb 16:33+, the dead are silent shadows of their former selves and can no longer speak with God, Is 38:18; Ps 30:9; 88:5, 10–12.

d. "I have grown old" Greek. The psalmist's "foes" regard the sick man's misfortune as a punishment for some hidden sin (cf. Job's friends). The theme is elaborated in other places (31; 35; 38; 69).

Psalm 7

a. Two protestations of innocence have been combined in this psalm. The first, vv. 1–5, 12b–16, in the wisdom style, demands strict retaliation; the second, vv. 6–12a, modeled on Jeremiah, appeals for the intervention of God the Judge. V. 17 is a liturgical conclusion.

b. The versions read "Cushite," cf. 2 S 18:21, the messenger who informed David of the death of Absalom. But "the Benjaminite" suggests one of David's enemies: Saul, Sheba or Shimei.

c. The law of *talio*, cf. Ex 21:25+, required that good be rendered for good, evil for evil. The text must not be watered down as in the versions "if I requited with evil the man who wronged me," or, "robbed (my persecutor)"; the morality of gospel times has yet to come, Mt 5:38f.

d. "me"; lit. "my soul," cf. 6:6+.

e. Lit. "my glory," but the word also means "liver," for the Semites the seat of thought and emotion. "Glory" also means "soul." The "dust" is that of the tomb.

f. "awake, my God" (Greek) comes after "enemies" in the text.

g. This gloss indicates that the peoples are gathered for judgment.

h. The text adds "that is on me."

i. "slow to (show his) anger" Greek; absent from Hebr.

j. These lines should follow v. 5; "enemy" has had, therefore, to be supplied.

k. The Hebr. verb *zamar*, Greek *psallein*, strictly means to play on a string instrument, or to sing with musical accompaniment.

Psalm 8

a. Possibly the harp, or a Philistine melody.

b. Corr. "may you (sing.) give" Hebr.

c. Christ quoted this text when the children had acclaimed his solemn entry into Jerusalem. In the liturgy it is used for the feast of the Holy Innocents (Mt 2:16).

d. I.e., the firmament or heavenly vault (Gn 1:6) on which stands the impregnable citadel from which God routs his foes (Mi 1:2; Ps 2:4; 150:1).

e. The author is thinking of man in comparison with the mysterious beings that constitute the court of Yahweh, Ps 29:1+, the "angels" of Greek and Vulg. Cf. Ps 45:6+.

f. Man, frail yet made in the likeness of God, on the border between the spiritual and material worlds, rules the natural creation.

Psalm 9

a. Ps 9 and 10 were originally one poem (as they are in Greek and Vulg.). The spokesman of the "poor," cf. Zp 2:3+, describes in a hymn and invokes in a prayer the execution of God's judgment on the wicked. The psalm is "alphabetical" (cf. Pr 31:10+) but in our present text, which is in a poor state, several letters have no corresponding strophe.

b. Translation uncertain.

c. The divine judgment is regarded as already given; the "day of Yahweh" will reveal its content. This eschatological theme is common in Ps.

d. "See" conj. Text uncertain.

e. Hebr. adds "because of those who hate me."

Psalm 10

a. Others translate "In his pride the wicked persecutes the poor."

b. Lit. "The grasping man blesses and spurns Yahweh, 4 the wicked, his anger on high . . ." We follow the Greek punctuation. Cf. v. 13. "blesses" is a euphemism as in 1 K 21:10, 13 and Jb 1:5, 11; 2:5, 9.

c. Denying the action of Providence, he speaks and acts as if there were no God at all.

d. "reeds" cf. Is 35:7; Hebr., wrongly vocalized, "settlements."

e. "questing of eye" absent from Hebr. "stoops" Greek. "into his power"; meaning uncertain.

f. To save, 138:7, and to strike, Mi 5:8; Is 11:15; Ezk 36:7.

g. Text uncertain.

Psalm 11

a. The faithful man is hunted like a bird, 55:6; 91:3; 124:7. The hill country is the place of refuge, Gn 19:17; Ezk 7:16; Ps 121:1; Mt 24:16.

b. "the world" versions.

c. "coals" Symmachus; "snares" Hebr.

d. Lit. "a scorching wind will be their cup-portion." This is a metaphor for destiny (the cup may have been used to contain lots), either happy (16:5; 23:5) or more frequently unhappy (75:8; Mt 20:22; Rv 14:10; 16:19); the cup of divine anger is one of the prophetic themes, Jr 25:15; Hg 2:16; Ezk 23:31f; Is 51:17+; Lm 4:21.

e. Corr.; the Hebr. reading "his face will look on the upright" is perhaps the result of a theological scruple, since man cannot see God, cf. Ex 33:20+. Nevertheless, the expression "to contemplate God's face" is common in Ps in the sense of standing in the presence of God like servants before a kindly master (15:1), cf. 16:11; 17:15; 24:6; 27:8+; 105:4; Is 38:11; Gn 33:10; Jb 33:26.

Psalm 12

a. Prayer in the manner of the prophets. Human deceit is contrasted with God's reliability in word and promise.

b. Lit. "smelted at the going into the earth," i.e. already refined when found. God's word is pure of any deceit.

c. Lit. "like a mound."

Psalm 13

a. Greek and Vulg. add "Let me sing to the name of Yahweh the Most High." Cf. 7:17.

Psalm 14

a. The "godless" man, cf. 10:4+, is a fool. His hour will come. Cf. Jr 5:12f.

b. Certain Greek MSS and Vulg. insert three verses here, quoted in Rm 3:10–18; they are to be found in 5:9; 140:3; 10:7; Pr 1:16; Is 59:7–8; Ps 36:1.

c. Figure of speech derived from the prophets.

d. Lit. "where there was no dread" (Greek and 53) absent from Hebr. Either such fear as has never been known before, or mysterious fear without apparent cause, cf. Lv 26:36; Dt 28:67; 1 S 14:15; 2 Ch 14:13; Jb 3:25.

e. The Hebr. verb (85:1; 126:1; Am 9:14; Ho 6:11; Jr 29:14, etc.; Ezk 16:53; Dt 30:3; Jb 42:10) means primarily the return from exile but frequently has the wider sense of re-establishing, restoring, changing the fortune.

Psalm 15

a. Summary of moral conduct, cf. the moral precepts of the Decalogue, Ex 20:1+.

b. God's loyal subjects. The phrase, common in Ps, is synonymous with "faithful," "pious," "devout." Later it is used for all in sympathy with Judaism, cf. Ac 2:11+; 10:2+.

Psalm 16

a. Meaning uncertain.

b. Vv. 2–3 are addressed to the psalmist's contemporaries who thought they could combine the worship of Yahweh as supreme god, v. 2, with that of local deities (lit. "holy ones," cf. 1 S 2:2), v. 3; such syncretism was Israel's great and persistent temptation. The translation changes (supported by the versions) only two vowels of the Hebr. text, keeping all the consonants.

c. Line corr. "idols," lit. "weaknesses" (euphemism).

d. Alluding to the levitical state. Their portion (the traditional "cup," cf. 11:6+, or "measuring line," Mi 2:4–5) is Yahweh. The name Hilkiah, "Yahweh-is-my-portion," is common.

e. Lit. "loins," like the heart, the seat of intimate thought and sentiment, cf. Jr 11:20; Pr 23:16; Ps 7:9.

f. Lit. "my glory," but cf. 7:5+.

g. The psalmist has set his heart on Yahweh. His lively faith and total commitment to God call for a union that defies dissolution, hence he must pray to escape death which would break that union, 6:5, cf. 49:15+. The hope, though vague as yet, is leading toward a belief in resurrection, Dn 12:2; 2 M 7:9+. The versions translate "pit" by "corruption." The text, which was applied to the Messiah in pre-Christian Judaism, finds its full sense in the resurrection of Christ.

Psalm 17
a. The text reads "our steps" at the beginning.

b. Text uncertain.

c. Lit. "from that which you hide." Scarcely a question of punishment here, as many think, but of passing pleasures to which the psalmist prefers God's friendship. "have all the sons they wish for" Greek.

d. The morning awakening is God's chosen hour for granting favors, 5:3; 30:5; 46:5; 49:14; 57:8; 73:20; 90:14; 130:6; 143:8. It is also the time when justice is done, 101:8+. Dawn and light are symbols of deliverance, Is 8:20; 9:1; 33:2; 58:10; Zp 3:5; Lm 3:23, cf. Jn 8:12+; evening and darkness symbolize trial and sorrow, Ps 17:3; Is 17:14; 50:10; Ps 30:5; 59:6; 88:18; 107:10. The word "awakening" has sometimes been taken as a subtle reference to the resurrection, cf. 2 K 4:31; Is 26:19; Dn 12:2 cf. Ps 16:10+.

Psalm 18
a. A triumphal ode combining a thanksgiving prayer, vv. 4–27, with a royal victory song, vv. 31–50, ending on a messianic note. Several textual corrections have been made in accordance with the parallel version in 2 S 22.

b. Line absent from Hebr.; 2 S 22 places it after v. 3.

c. In Ps God is often called the Rock of Israel, i.e. the bulwark of his people and especially of the Davidic dynasty. Cf. Mt 16:18+.

d. My strong defense. The "horn" is the symbol of strength.

e. "waves" 2 S; "cords, nets" Hebr. The waters symbolize deadly peril, 32:6; 40:2; 42:7; 66:12; 69:1f, 14f; 88:17, 130:1; Is 8:7; 30:28; Jb 22:11; 27:20; Jon 2:6.

f. God's triumphant intervention on behalf of the psalmist; the description of this theophany, vv. 7–17, now begins. Cf. Ex 13:22+; 19:16+.

g. The cherubs above the ark, Ex 25:18+, inspiring Ezekiel's vision of the Chariot of God, Ezk 1:3+; they form a throne for Yahweh, 1 S 4:4; 2 S 6:2; 2 K 19:15. From the destruction of the Temple onward they symbolize heavenly beings.

h. Following 2 S. The Hebr. softens the utilitarian metaphor "you light my lamp."

i. Lit. "your gentle care fosters me," cf. 71:21; Ezk 19:2.

Psalm 19

a. This hymn celebrates Yahweh as creator of the heavens, and particularly of the sun (vv. 4b–6), and the author of the Law; Nature and Law both manifest the perfection of God. In the ancient East the sun symbolized justice, cf. Ml 3:20; Ws 5:6; hence the conjunction of the psalm's two sections. The Christmas liturgy applies the psalm to the Word of God, the Sun of Righteousness, Ml 3:20; Jn 1:9; Lk 1:78. V. 4 is applied to the apostles, cf. Rm 10:18.

b. The versions interpret "(theirs is not a language) whose sound cannot be heard"; but in what follows there is allusion to the Assyro-Babylonian idea that the stars are the silent "writing of the heavens."

c. The psalmist, speaking of the sun as a creature of God, uses expressions found also in Babylonian mythology.

d. "his words" corr.; "plentiful and" Hebr.

e. "from pride," lit. "from proud men" (or "proud things"); Greek "alien (gods)," cf. Jr 3:13 (false gods). Ps 119 persistently contrasts pride with obedience to the Law.

f. "always" Greek.

g. In Hebr. goel. Originally meaning the avenger of blood, cf. Nb 35:19+, the word is used of Yahweh as avenger, savior, and rescuer of his servants and his people from death, in Is (41:14; 44:6), and in the psalms, 9:12; 49:7, 15; 69:18; 72:14; 74:2; 77:15; 103:4; 107:2.

Psalm 20

a. Prayer for the king as he sets out to war, cf. 1 K 8:44; 2 Ch 20:18f. Each of the two sections is followed by a choral antiphon.

b. "his anointed" (Greek *christos*), cf. Ex 30:22+; 1 S 9:26+: the king of Israel.

c. "answer us" versions; "he answers us" Hebr.

Psalm 21

a. This psalm of two sections followed by choral antiphons, vv. 7 and 13, strikes a messianic and eschatological note, and for this reason is applied to Christ the King.

b. Lit. "in the day of your face," i.e. when you come to judge. Vv. 8–12 are addressed to the king, but the expression "the day of your face" and the mention of fire suggest a more distant, eschatological perspective. It is impossible that in the original text this passage was addressed to Yahweh (cf. Greek MSS).

Psalm 22

a. This lament and entreaty of an innocent man under persecution ends in thanksgiving for his rescue, vv. 22–26, and deserves its place in the national liturgy by virtue of v. 23 and its conclusion, vv. 27–31, where the coming of the kingdom of God throughout the world seems to result from the ordeal of the faithful servant. Reminiscent of the poem of the suffering servant in Is 52:13–53:12, this psalm, the opening line of which was spoken by Christ on the cross, and into which the evangelists read an anticipatory description of several episodes in the Passion, is messianic at least in the typical sense.

b. Possibly the first words of a familiar song. Versions "For morning solace."

c. Or "You who dwell in the sanctuary, the praise of Israel," cf. Greek.

d. "He relied on" versions; "Rely on" Hebr.

e. "palate" corr.; "strength" Hebr.

f. "tie" Symmachus and Jerome. Hebr. uncertain "like a lion"; Greek "have dug into"; Syr. "have wounded"; Vulg. "have pierced." The passage recalls Is 53:5 but the evangelists have not made use of it in the Passion narratives.

g. "(they) leave me" corr.; "you leave me" Hebr.

h. Versions "They count."

i. "my poor (soul)" conj. following versions; "you have answered me" Hebr.

j. Allusion to the messianic banquet, Is 55:1f, etc., rather than to the ritual meal following the communion sacrifice, Lv. 3:1+.

k. "their" Greek; "your" Hebr.

l. "him" versions; "thee" Hebr.

m. "Before him" corr.; "they will eat" Hebr. "my soul will live for him, my . . ." versions; "who does not keep his soul alive, a . . ." Hebr.

n. "still to come" Greek; "they will come" Hebr.

o. A common phrase in the second part of Is (41:20; 42:16, etc.)

Psalm 23

a. The care of God for the righteous, illustrated by two images: the shepherd, vv. 1–4, and the host of the messianic banquet, vv. 5–6. The psalm is traditionally applied to the sacramental life, particularly to baptism and the Eucharist.

b. Hebr. inserts "you are" before "beside me."

c. Gesture of hospitality in the East, Am 6:6; Ps 92:10; 133:2; Qo 9:8; Lk 7:46.

d. "my home" versions; "I shall return to" Hebr.

Psalm 24

a. Possibly vv. 7–10 refer to the translation of the ark in the days of David, 2 S 6:12–16, cf. Ps 68:24f; 132. The first part, vv. 1–6, seems to be of later date, cf. Ps 15: the creator of the universe is also the befriender of the upright.

b. The earth is represented as resting on the waters of the nether ocean (cf. Ex 20:4).

c. "God of Jacob" Syr.; "of the God of Jacob" Greek; "Jacob" Hebr.

Psalm 25

a. The sages of Israel had taught that the righteous man would receive reward on earth; to this is now added the hope, nursed by those back from exile, of the unconditional enjoyment of the land of their ancestors.

b. Not so much the mystery of God himself, Ws 2:22, as an intimacy with God, 73:28; Pr 3:32; Jb 29:5; Ex 33:20+, together with an understanding of the ways of God, Jr 16:21; 31:34; Ho 6:6.

c. "relieve" corr.; "they have relieved" Hebr.; "are multiplied" Greek.

Psalm 26

a. As in 7 and 17 the believer protests his innocence.

b. Hebr. adds "Yahweh."

c. Hebr. adds "Yahweh" at the beginning. Hebr. "the beauty of your house"; "beauty" Greek.

d. "Yahweh" Greek; omitted by Hebr.

e. "you" Greek; omitted by Hebr.

Psalm 27

a. "awning" and "tent": the Temple in Jerusalem.

b. "seek (sing.) his face" corr.; "seek (plur.) my face" Hebr. This expression, cf. Am 5:4+, originally signifying "to consult Yahweh" in his sanctuary, 2 S 21:1, took on a wider sense: to seek to know God to live in his presence. To "seek God," Dt 4:29; Ps 40:16; 69:6; 105:3, etc., is to serve him faithfully. Cf. Am 5:4+.

c. Or "Oh, if I were sure of seeing!"

Psalm 28

a. "Yahweh" here and in v. 4 is absent from Hebr.

b. "my flesh has bloomed again" Greek.

c. The parallelism suggests that the "anointed" is here the people of God consecrated to his service, cf. Ex 19:6+; Hab 3:13; Ps 105:15, and not the king, 20:6, or the high priest, 84:9.

Psalm 29

a. The tempest, cf. Ex 13:22+ and Ex 19:16+, evokes the glory and power of God, subduing the enemies of Israel and assuring peace to the Chosen People.

b. Lit. "sons of the gods," cf. 82:1; 89:6; Jb 1:6+, i.e. the angels who constitute the heavenly court. The passage is sometimes applied to Israel, the "son of God," Ex 4:22; Dt 14:1; Ho 11:1. After this line Greek and Vulg. add "Bring sons of rams to Yahweh."

c. "court" versions; "adornments" Hebr. The "sacred court" is heaven, invisible counterpart of the Temple of Jerusalem, 11:4; 78:69.

d. Sidonian name for Lebanon, Dt 3:9.

e. God sharpens arrows to transfix his enemies, cf. 18:14; Dt 32:23, 42; Hab 3:11; Zc 9:14.

f. "the terebinths" corr.; "(makes) the hinds (calve)" Hebr. The tall trees, here and in v. 5, perhaps symbolize the proud enemies of God and of his people, cf. Is 2:13; 10:18, 33; 32:19; Jr 21:14; 46:23; Ezk 21:2; Zc 11:2.

g. Either in heaven, v. 2, or in the Temple where the liturgy echoes the praise of the heavenly court, or else in the Holy Land, consecrated to Yahweh, 114:2, and his dwelling place, Jr 12:7; Zc 9:8.

h. The Flood was the first great act of God's triumphant justice which will be always exercised on behalf of his people.

Psalm 30

a. Lit. "in the evening, tears pass the night."

b. Text corr.; "on my mountain you have set up a fortress" Hebr. Allusion to Zion, or a metaphor of safety.

c. "my God" Greek; "Lord" Hebr.

d. I.e. my death; life resides in the blood, Gn 9:6+; Lv 1:5+; Ps 72:14 and 116:15.

Psalm 31

a. "rescue" Greek; it is put after "make haste" in Hebr.

b. "you hate" versions; "I hate" Hebr.

c. "misery" versions; "iniquity" Hebr.

d. "loathsome" corr.; "exceedingly" Hebr.

e. "Yahweh" versions; absent from Hebr.

f. Scorn, slander, perjury; Jr 18:18; Is 54:17; 1 K 21:10, 13; Jb 5:21; Ps 55:9; 109:3; 120:2f.

g. "snatched" corr.

Psalm 32

a. A didactic poem; its two parts, vv. 1–7 and 8–11, balance each other but the rhythm is different. One of the Penitential Psalms.

b. Lit. "his sin is covered," cf. 65:3+; 85:2; Jb 31:33.

c. "my heart" one MS; absent from Text. Rec. "stubble" corr.

d. "have pardoned" corr.; "Selah" (i.e. Pause) Hebr.

e. "of trouble" corr.

f. "songs" doubtful word.

g. Word translated from corresponding Arabic.

Psalm 33

a. This word originally indicated the war cry that preluded attack, Ex 32:17; Jos 6:5; Jg 7:20–21; 1 S 17:20, 52; Am 1:14; 2:2; Ho 5:8; Jr 4:19; 49:2; it hailed Yahweh as king and leader, Nb 23:21; Zp 1:16; cf. 1 S 10:24, and his palladium, the ark, 1 S 4:5; 2 S 6:15. After the Exile this ritual war cry assumes a ceremonial and liturgical character: it acclaims Yahweh as king of Israel and of the nations, 47:1, 5; 89:15; 95:1; 98:4, 6, as savior, Is 44:23, and as judge, Jl 2:1; it hails his Messiah also, Zc 9:9. It is shouted on feast days, Ezr 3:11, cf. Jb 38:7, at thanksgiving sacrifices, 27:6; 65:13; 100:1; and in religious processions, 95:1; 100:1f.

b. "wineskin" versions; "heap" Hebr.

Psalm 34

a. Wisdom and "alphabetical" psalm, cf. Pr 31:10+ (though the sequence of strophes is upset): a thanksgiving, vv. 1–10, and an instruction (in the style of Pr) on the fates of the upright and the wicked, vv. 11–22.

b. "The young lion"; Hebr. reads plural; Greek "The rich."

c. Versions "The death of the wicked is an evil one."

Psalm 35

a. A long lament and imprecation; akin to 22, 55, 59, 69, 70, 109.

b. "pike" conj.; "halt (them)" Hebr.

c. Text corrected following Syr.

d. "strangers" conj.; "smitten ones" (or "cripples") Hebr.

e. Following Greek. Hebr. corrupt.

f. Word uncertain.

g. "with the," lit. "even against the"; "and in anger" Greek.

h. Falsely accusing him of some crime.

Psalm 36

a. The two parts of this psalm, vv. 1–4; 5–12, may have existed separately.

b. For the wicked, the voice of Sin here personified, takes the place of the word of God.

c. Text uncertain.

d. I.e. the high mountains, cf. 68:15; 80:10.

e. Rhythm disturbed, text doubtful.

f. "life" means prosperity, peace, happiness, cf. 133:3. The "fountain of life" in Pr is wisdom, Pr 13:14; 16:22; 18:4, and the fear of God, 14:27. This passage is applied to Christ, the life and light of men, cf. Jn *passim*.

g. The "light of the face" of God, 27:1; 89:15; Jb 29:3, is his benevolence, cf. 4:6+; in it man finds the "light" of happiness.

Psalm 37

a. This "alphabetical" psalm, "A mirror of Providence" (Tertullian) counters the indignation of those outraged by the prosperity of the ungodly with the teachings of the sages on earthly rewards and punishments for the upright and the wicked respectively. The debate is continued in Qo (8:11–14) and Jb.

b. The Holy Land, cf. 25:13; Dt 16:20. "live in peace," lit. "feed securely," cf. Is 14:30. The Beatitudes give these promises a spiritual sense, Mt 5:3–4, cf. Rm 4:13.

c. With versions; "the wealth of many wicked" Hebr.

d. Greek "those who bless him . . . those who curse him"; Syr. adds "Yahweh."

e. Greek; absent from Hebr. "perish" Greek; "be preserved" Hebr.

f. Corr. according to Greek.

g. "I" versions; "he" Hebr.

Psalm 38

a. Complaint of a devout man who is sick and therefore assumed to be sinful, cf. vv. 3–4, 5b, 18. Penitential Psalm. Some passages are reminiscent of Jb and the poem of the suffering servant, Is 53.

b. "pressed down" Syr.; "fallen" Hebr.

c. "for no reason" corr.; "living" Hebr.

d. Some Greek MSS and versions add, "They have rejected me, the loved one, like a hideous corpse" (cf. Is 14:19), an allusion to the crucified Christ; the Coptic version, still more explicitly, "They have nailed my flesh."

Psalm 39

a. Cf. 88. The psalmist expresses his dismay at the prosperity of the godless and the shortness of life, vv. 1–6; he commends himself to God and begs for his favor.

b. Corr. (lit. "because of his good").

c. "wealth" corr.; "they are in turmoil" Hebr.

d. Lit. "that I may look cheerful," cf. Jb 9:27; 10:20.

Psalm 40

a. The hymn of thanksgiving, vv. 1–11, is followed by a cry of distress, vv. 13–17, identical with Ps 70. In the present arrangement the first part seems to be a review of past happiness as contrasted with present misery, leading up to the appeal to Yahweh.

b. Lit. "dug out." God sees to it that his servant knows his will, cf. Is 50:5. A Greek variant, "you have fashioned a body for me," was interpreted messianically and applied to Christ, Heb 10:5f.

c. Obedience is better than sacrifice, 1 S 15:22. The "book" is the Law. "am I not commanded" lit. "it is laid down for me"; the Jewish textual tradition punctuates differently, so also Greek which translates "it is written of me," suggesting a messianic meaning.

d. Cf. Ps 70; or read with Text "the Lord will think of me."

Psalm 41
a. "the poor" Greek.
b. "give him happiness" versions.
c. Text uncertain.
d. Sickness is regarded as a punishment for sin, cf. Jb; Ps 38:3; 107:17.
e. Lit. "thing of Belial," cf. Dt 13:14+.
f. Lit. "lifts the heel against me." Jesus applied this text to Judas.
g. This doxology closes the first book of the Psalter.

Psalm 42
a. Exile, a symbol of the troubles of the devout, "exiled far from the Lord," 2 Co 5:6–8, here means absence from the Temple which is God's dwelling place, and from the festivals uniting his people there.
b. "doe" Greek; "hart" Hebr., but the verb is feminine.
c. "to see" versions. "To see the face of God" (cf. Hebr. "appear before") here means to visit his sanctuary, the Temple in Jerusalem, cf. Dt 31:11; Ps 27:8+. For the primary meaning of the phrase, cf. Ex 33:20+.
d. "wonderful" Greek and Syr.; Hebr. uncertain (corr. "in stately procession"). The "Tent" was the desert sanctuary of ancient times; its memory was recalled annually by the "feast of Tents," or "of Tabernacles," Ex 23:14+; here the word is used for its successor, the Temple, God's dwelling place, the object of yearly pilgrimage for every devout Israelite, Ex 23:14.
e. Lit. "salvation of my face" corr., cf. v. 11.
f. "you, humble mountain" corr. referring to Mount Zion. Hebr. "from the lowly mountain" or "from Mount Misar," alluding to Zaorah not far from the sources of Jordan; the "you" would then refer to God.
g. Corr. (lit. "with a rending cry in my bones").

Psalm 43
a. Hebr. here adds "God." In the Roman rite, Ps 43 was formerly said at the beginning of the Mass.
b. "my joy" one MS; "the joy (of my delight)." Text. Rec. Greek interprets "God who makes joyful my youth."

Psalm 44
a. This psalm contrasting past victories with present humiliations

246

may, like 74, 79, 80, refer to the destruction of Jerusalem in 587. Vv. 17–22 have perhaps been added later to adapt the psalm to the persecutions of the Maccabaean period.

b. "by" corr.

c. Lit. "a shaking of the head for the peoples."

d. Either the devastated country, Is 34:13; Jr 9:10, or the desert, a refuge for persecuted Jews, 1 M 2:29; 9:33.

e. Attitude of prayer, 28:2; 141:2; Is 1:15.

Psalm 45

a. According to some scholars, this psalm may be a secular song to celebrate the marriage of an Israelite king, Solomon, Jeroboam II, or Ahab (whose bride was a Tyrian princess, 1 K 16:31). But Jewish and Christian tradition understand it as celebrating the marriage of the messianic King with Israel (prefiguring the Church), cf. Ezk 16:8–13; Is 62:5; Sg 3:11, etc., and the liturgy develops the allegory still further by applying it to our Lady and to the Virgin Saints. The poet first addresses the messianic King, vv. 2–9, crediting him with attributes of Yahweh (145:4–7, 12–13, etc.) and of Immanuel (Is 9:5–6); he then addresses the queen, vv. 10–16.

b. Possibly "On the six-stringed lute."

c. "Stretch tight" versions; "and your majesty" Hebr. (which has this at the beginning of the verse). "bowstring" corr.; "and teach you" Hebr.

d. In the Bible the title "God" is given to the angels, 8:5+, to leaders and judges, 58:1+, to Moses, Ex 4:16; 7:1, to the ghost of Samuel, 1 S 28:13+, to the House of David, Zc 12:8, to the Messiah, Is 9:5.

e. "waft from" corr.

f. In the interpretation of this psalm as the marriage of the messianic King, this is a reference to the pagan nations converted to the true God, Is 60:3f; 61:5; Sg 1:3; 6:8, and following Israel into his service, vv. 14–15.

g. In the messianic interpretation: Israel, like the ancestral figure Abraham, must sever all links with the surrounding pagan world, thus leaving the "ancestral home" in order to receive "sons," v. 16.

h. In the messianic interpretation: the homage of the pagan peoples as prophesied for the messianic age.

i. "Dressed" versions; "her dress" Hebr. Before "set" Hebr. has "the king's daughter within."

j. "Her" corr.; "your" Hebr.

Psalm 46

a. Canticle of Zion. God's presence in the Temple safeguards the Holy City, while symbolic waters purify and fertilize it, making it a second Eden.

b. Images of a return of chaos. The earth rests on the waters of the nether ocean, 24:2, being supported by pillars, cf. Jb 9:6; Ps 75:3; 104:5; Pr 8:27; when these are shaken the waters are released and dash against the mountains.

c. The refrain, here missing from the text, is restored from vv. 7 and 11.

d. "sanctifies" Greek; "the (most) holy (of dwellings)" Hebr.

e. Hour of God's favor, 17:15+. Probable allusion to the withdrawal of Sennacherib's forces in 701, 2 K 19:35; Is 17:14.

f. "shields" Greek; "chariots" Hebr.

Psalm 47

a. Eschatological hymn; first of the "Psalms of Kingship," cf. 93f; it elaborates the acclamation, "Yahweh is King!" The King of Israel goes up to the Temple in triumphal procession to the sound of ritual acclamation, 33:3+. His empire extends to all nations who will one day join the Chosen People.

b. "our" Greek.

c. "to" versions; absent from Hebr. The covenant with Abraham is extended to the whole human race. The "shields" are the kings, defenders of their peoples.

Psalm 48

a. A hymn extolling Mount Zion, the nucleus of ancient Jerusalem, site of the royal palace and the Temple, cf. 2 S 5:9+. It may contain an allusion, vv. 4 and 5, to the defeat of the Syro-Ephraimitic alliance against Ahaz in 735 and the hasty retreat of Sennacherib in 701.

b. In Phoenician poetry "the mountain of the North" is the home of the gods; the psalmist adopts the expression, applying it to Mount Zion.

c. Seagoing vessels capable of sailing to "Tarshish," cf. Is 23:1+.

d. The neighboring towns.

e. The psalm may date from the rebuilding of the walls by Nehemiah, Ne 6:15; 12:27.

f. Hebr. adds "to death," a corrupt rubric belonging to the following psalm.

Psalm 49

a. Like 37 and 73, this psalm deals with the problem of retribution and the apparent prosperity of the godless, resolving it in the traditional fashion of the sages. An ironical dictum provides the theme, vv. 12 and 20.

b. "dogs my steps and" (lit. "of those who dog my steps"), cf. Hexapla.

c. "tombs" versions; "inside" Hebr.

d. "forfeits intelligence" versions, cf. v. 20; "does not endure" Hebr.

e. Translation uncertain.

f. Here personified, cf. Ho 13:14; Jr 9:20; Jb 18:13; 28:22.

g. The hour for eschatological judgments and the triumph of the upright, cf. 17:15+. Text of v. 14 uncertain.

h. The psalmist trusts God to keep him beyond the reach of Sheol. It cannot be asserted that here he glimpses the possibility of being "taken up" to heaven like Enoch and Elijah, cf. 16:10+; 73:24; but he does think that the ultimate fate of the upright must differ from that of the godless and that the friendship of God can have no end. This implicit faith in a retribution to come prepares for the later revelation of the resurrection of the dead, and eternal life, 2 M 7:9+.

i. In contrast, God will glorify the upright, 73:24; 91:15.

Psalm 50

a. God comes to judge Israel, vv. 1–7; he arraigns the formalism of sacrifice, vv. 8–15, accompanied by contempt for the commandments, vv. 16–23.

b. "my mountains" corr.; "mountains (in thousands)" Hebr.

c. Lit. "heavens" versions; "mountains" Hebr.

d. So far God has addressed all Israel indiscriminately; this line may have been added to exclude the virtuous from what follows.

e. "upright man" corr.

Psalm 51

a. Penitential Psalm (cf. 6:1+) with close affinity to prophetic literature, especially Is and Ezk.

b. Sin, though God does not prevent it, calls down divine judgment. Some translate "that you may be found just . . ."

c. Man is born in a state of impurity, Jb 14:4+, cf. Pr 20:9, which is an implicit recognition of his tendency to evil, Gn 8:21. This basic impurity is here pleaded as a mitigating circumstance, cf.

249

1 K 8:46, which God should take into account. The doctrine of original sin will be proposed explicitly, Rm 5:12–21, in connection with the revelation of redemption by Jesus Christ.

d. Translation following versions; Hebr. "in the secret (place) teach me wisdom." This wisdom will enable man to discover the hidden faults of which he is unaware, 19:12; Jb 11:6.

e. Plant used for sprinkling in purifications, Lv 14:4; Nb 19:18.

f. This verb always has God for its subject; it designates the act by which he brings something new and wonderful into being, Gn 1:1; Is 48:7; 65:17; Jr 31:21–22; Ex 34:10. The justification of the sinner is the most wonderful of all the works of God, and is analogous to the act of creation, cf. Ezk 36:25f. Cf. also Jr 31:33; 32:39–40.

g. Here considered as the principle (within man but given by God) of moral and religious activity, whether of the individual, 143:10; Ws 1:5; 9:17, or of the nation as a whole, Is 63:11; Hg 2:5; Ne 9:20.

h. Lit. "blood spilt." The reference here is to premature death, which according to traditional teaching was the punishment for sin, rather than to the murder of Uriah (2 S 12:9, 13), or to future crimes in which the psalmist might be involved whether as agent or as victim. Hebr. adds "O God" before "God my savior."

i. "My sacrifice" corr.; "God's sacrifices" Hebr. The Hebr. adds "O God" to the following line.

j. After the return from exile the rebuilding of the walls of Jerusalem was eagerly looked forward to as a sign of divine forgiveness, Jr 30:15–18; Ezk 36:33.

k. Liturgical annotation; inserted later. In the restored Jerusalem sacrifice will recover its value because it will be offered with devotion (lit. "righteous sacrifice").

Psalm 52
a. The translation follows the Greek. Hebr. "Tyrant, the kindness of God (lasts) the whole day long."

Psalm 53
a. "Elohistic" edition of 14, where see notes.

b. "the apostate" versions; "him who besieges you" Hebr. The text of this verse seems less corrupt than in 14.

Psalm 54
a. The name as substitute for the person, cf. Ex 3:14+.

b. "Arrogant men"; var. "strangers."

Psalm 55

    a. Meaning uncertain.

    b. Text corr.

    c. "Were it" Greek; "It is not" Hebr.

    d. "May they recoil" corr.; "we went" Hebr.

    e. Sudden, premature death is the punishment of the wicked, 73:19; 102:24; Is 38:10; Jr 17:11; Jb 15:32.

    f. The hours of prayer, Dn 6:11.

    g. I.e. the "friend" of v. 13.

    h. This verse may be understood as the ironical remarks of the false friend, or as self-encouragement uttered by the sufferer.

Psalm 56

    a. "of the gods" cf. Greek and 58:1.

    b. "Raise me up" corr.

    c. Here, as in v. 10, the "word" of God is his promise on which his servant relies, cf. 106:12; 119:42, 65; 130:5.

    d. "are they to go unpunished?" lit. "deliverance for them"; the versions interpret "for nothing you will deliver them."

    e. This line, possibly an addition, brings the idea of a general judgment of all nations (cf. 79; 9:5, etc.) into the psalmist's narrower perspective of a judgment on his particular enemies.

    f. The text adds a tentative gloss "Should this not be: 'in your book'?", cf. Jb 19:23; Ml 3:16; Ps 139:16.

    g. Lit. "my soul from Death"; Hebr. adds "should this not be: 'my feet from death'?"; some Greek MSS "my eyes from tears," cf. v. 8 and 116:8.

Psalm 57

    a. The psalmist wants God to manifest his sovereignty by rescuing the oppressed and destroying the godless.

    b. Personified as in Jb 3:9; 38:12; 41:10. Dawn is the hour of rescue, 17:15+.

Psalm 58

    a. Like the prophets of old the poet apostrophizes unjust judges, and calls divine judgment down on them.

    b. "Gods" corr.; "in silence" Hebr. The expression here embraces judges and rulers. Cf. Ex 21:6; 22:7; Dt 19:17; 2 S 14:17; Ps 45:6; 82.

    c. Lit. "untimely birth of a woman"; "of a woman" Greek, Syr.; other readings "fire," "and the mole."

d. Corr. following Symmachus and Jerome.

Psalm 59

a. This psalm with its mixture of praise and imprecation has two refrains: vv. 6 and 14; 9 and 17. The author may have been a Jew of the Dispersion, surrounded by hostile pagans, or a devout man living in a half-paganized Jerusalem.

b. Eschatological style, cf. Is 26:21.

c. The image suggests, cf. vv. 14–15, the packs of stray dogs found in the villages of the East.

d. A form of blasphemy, cf. 10:4; 14:1; 64:5; 94:7.

e. "My Strength": MSS and versions, cf. v. 17; "his strength"; "who loves me," lit. "of my love": MSS and versions, "his love": Text. Rec.

f. "Slaughter them" corr., cf. v. 13a; "do not slaughter them" Hebr., cf. Ezk 12:16.

g. "growling" versions; "spending the night" Hebr.

Psalm 60

a. This psalm implies the same historical situation as 44 and 80. V. 5 introduces an oracle of hope, repeated in 108:6–13, foretelling the restoration of an enlarged and unified kingdom, as in the early days of the monarchy, with control over Edom, Ephraim, Gilead, cf. Ob; Is 11:13–14.

b. The defeat is described in apocalyptic terms.

c. The banner, or rallying signal, is a common feature (Ex 17:15; Is 5:26; 11:10; 49:22; 62:10; Sg 2:4); here however it is the signal for retreat, cf. v. 10.

d. Or "by his holiness," i.e. guaranteeing his promises.

e. An ancient custom, Dt 25:9; in Rt 4:7+, it signifies appropriation.

f. Ironical; 108:9 "and shout, 'Victory!' over Philistia."

g. Hebr. repeats "God."

Psalm 61

a. Lament of a Levite in exile from Mt. Zion, vv. 1–5, followed by a prayer for the king, vv. 6–7.

b. Others translate "that is higher than I."

c. These personified divine attributes will accompany the messianic King, 85:10f; 89:14, 24, as they protect the king, Pr 20:28, or the faithful Levite, Ps 40:11. Vv. 6–7 may be an ancient prayer for the king, but their emphasis on a reign indefinitely prolonged recalls the prophecy of Nathan, 2 S 7:16; 1 Ch 17:14, and their close resemblance to the messianic passages of Ps 72 and 89 makes them applicable to the royal Messiah.

Psalm 62

a. Didactic psalm: human malice, hollowness of things created, vanity of riches, impartiality of the divine judge. The theme of the refrain, vv. 1–2, 5–6, is that of the following psalm.

b. "Deceit" corr.; "from his eminence" Hebr.

c. Lit. "sons of Adam," "sons of men," ordinary people and men of rank respectively, as in 49:2.

d. The literary device of "numerical proverbs" is found in Am 1:3f; Pr 6:16; 30:15; Jb 40:5.

e. Doctrine of individual retribution taught by the prophets (especially Ezekiel, 14:12+), the wisdom writers and the psalmists, 37:1+.

Psalm 63

a. Versions "from early morning I am with you."

b. By Yahweh, cf. Jr 12:16; Dt 6:13; or by the king: the text is ambiguous.

Psalm 64

a. By the law of retaliation, the arrow of God, v. 7, avenges the arrow of the wicked word, v. 3.

b. Text corr. Hebr. "they search out (contrive) wicked deeds; we are ready (MSS: they hide), a plot they hatch; and the depths."

c. Lit. "make them stumble" corr.

Psalm 65

a. After a good year with plentiful rain the people thank the creator. The first part, vv. 1–8, with its worldwide outlook, is reminiscent of Is. The second, vv. 9–13, with a change of rhythm in v. 10, is an enthusiastic description of spring in Judah.

b. Lit. "is due to you" versions; "silence (is praise)" Hebr.

c. "blot out" lit. "cover the sin": expression in the "Priestly" vocabulary for divine pardon, granted especially on the Day of Atonement, Lv 16+; cf. Ps 78:38; 79:9.

d. "islands" Targum; "sea" Hebr.

e. "are in uproar" Greek; "and the uproar (of the nations)" Hebr.

f. These gates through which the sun was thought to pass each day represent the most distant countries.

g. "water it" versions; "make it overflow" Hebr.

h. Others translate "A channel, God, is filled with water." The poet is thinking of the storehouses above the firmament where the waters are kept, Gn 1:7; Ps 104:3; Jb 38:25, not the symbolic river of Zion, 46:4+.

i. The chariot of God, 68:4, 17; Is 66:5, traverses the earth dispensing fertility.

j. Lit. "they acclaim, yes they sing."

Psalm 66

a. This liturgical thanksgiving on behalf of the community, the leader of which speaks from v. 13 onward, recalls in style and worldwide outlook the second half of Is.

b. The crossing of the Red Sea, Ex 14–15, and of the Jordan, Jos 3: two great "typical" events of Israel's history, also found together in 74:13–15; 114.

c. Hence the title "Resurrection Psalm" given to this psalm by some Greek MSS and Vulg. The Easter liturgy uses this verse.

d. "To draw breath" versions; "to abundance" Hebr.

Psalm 67

a. Probably recited at the harvest-home festival, cf. Ex 23:14+.

b. This refrain is in the spirit of the second part of Is: by the example of the Chosen People and the lessons of its history the pagan nations also are summoned to serve the one God.

c. Lit. "you judge the world with justice, you judge"; "the world . . . judge" Sinaiticus; omitted by Hebr.

Psalm 68

a. This hymn of thanksgiving covers the chief stages in the history of the people of God, like those of a triumphal progress by Yahweh: the Exodus from Egypt, the journey through the desert, the victories of the period of the Judges (Deborah, Gideon), the installation of the ark on Zion, the story of Elijah and Elisha, the tragic fate of the family of Ahab, the solemn Passover of Hezekiah, and finally the worldwide perspectives of the closing chapters of Is. Between Prelude (vv. 1–6) and Conclusion (vv. 32–35) are six groups of two strophes, the strophes being paired off on the basis of subject matter. A copyist's error has upset the order of strophes 6 and 7.

b. "they disperse" versions; "you disperse them" Hebr.

c. "rejoice" corr.; "in his name" Hebr.

d. Hebr. gloss "that is, Sinai," as in Jg 5:5. This strophe shows Yahweh taking the field; his departure from Egypt in the cloud, Ex 13:21; Nb 14:14, and the theophany of Sinai, Ex 19:16+.

e. The miracles of the Exodus: the manna, the quails and the entry into the Promised Land.

f. Hebr. divides differently "the couriers are a huge army."

g. The victories of the conquest. "Women" (lit. "fair one") means possibly Jael, Jg 5:24, or perhaps the wives of the conquerors, cf. Jg 5:30; 11:34; 1 S 18:6.

h. Lit. "in the middle of the two walls" (leading in to the sheepfold); some translate "between the hearthstones" or "between the two panniers" (carried by a donkey), cf. Gn 49:14.

i. Text corr. The Hebr. of v. 14 has "When Shaddai routed the kings on it (fem.) snow fell on Dark Mountain." "Dark Mountain" is probably a wooded hill near Shechem (cf. Jg 9:48–49). In imitation of Jg 5:16f, the poet here seems to address the uncooperative clans who took no part in the fighting. He jibes at them with his boast of abundant spoil (cf. Jos 22:8; Jg 8:26) which the womenfolk divide: the precious stones gleam on their dusky skin (cf. Sg 1:5) like a dove's plumage or like snow on dark ground (Sg 2:14; Lm 4:7).

j. The hill of Zion, God's dwelling place on earth, 2 S 5:9+.

k. Not the chariots of Solomon, 1 K 10:26, but the heavenly chariots seen by Elisha, 2 K 6:17; cf. 7:6; Is 66:15. What follows refers to the victories of the monarchical period.

l. "has left . . ." corr.; "in them, Sinai in the sanctuary" Hebr.

m. Zion.

n. "O God" follows "Yahweh" in Hebr. Text uncertain.

o. Allusion to the death of Ahab, 1 K 21:19; 22:38, of Jehoram, 2 K 9:24, and of Jezebel, 2 K 9:36.

p. Liturgical antiphon. For "you who spring from" (lit. "fountain") some suggest the similar Hebr. word for "assembly."

q. Meaning doubtful.

r. Vv. 24–27 refer to the Passover of Hezekiah, 2 Ch 30, in which the N. tribes took part.

s. Text corr., cf. versions; "your God has commanded your strength" Hebr. The text and rhythm of the two following strophes are rather uncertain.

t. Alluding to Egypt. The "bulls" and "calves" are leaders and people.

u. Lit. "great men" corr.; "bronze(?)" Hebr. "stretch out" corr.

v. Hebr. adds "the Lord. Pause."

w. "his sanctuary" cf. versions; "your sanctuary" or "your sanctuaries" Hebr.

Psalm 69

a. This psalm is composed of two laments of differing rhythms, each containing a lamentation followed by a prayer. The first, vv.

1–6 and 13–15, elaborates the themes of the nether waters, 18:4+, and enemies, 35 etc. The second, vv. 7–12 and 16f, is a cry of distress of a devout man who suffers for his zeal, cf. Is 53:10; Jr 15:15; Ps 22. The psalm ends as a hymn of national application, vv. 30f, cf. 22:27f and 102:13f. The messianic character of the psalm is brought out by the use made of it in the N.T.

b. Or "up to my soul."

c. Lit. "than my tresses" corr.; "those who would destroy me" Hebr.

d. This line, recalling Lv 5:23, has perhaps been added.

e. Hebr. inserts "Lord" before "Yahweh."

f. Lit. "humble" cf. versions; "weep" Hebr.

g. "are past cure" corr.; "I tremble" Hebr.

h. "adding" versions; "recounting" Hebr. The object of persecution in v. 26 is plural in Hebr., adapting the psalm to liturgical use.

Psalm 70

a. Doublet of 40:13–17, where see notes.

Psalm 71

a. "sheltering" ("of security") MSS, versions. "a walled fortress" Greek and 31:2.

b. Meaning uncertain (versions "my strength"?).

c. Because of his sufferings: they are surprised to see a good man suffer, cf. Jb.

d. Hebr. adds "I have not known how to read the letters," doubtless the gloss of a scribe puzzled by the following word.

e. Meaning uncertain; possibly "strengthened by Yahweh I shall come (into the sanctuary)." Hebr. inserts "Lord" before "Yahweh."

f. This passage could be applied to Israel, whose "youth" and "old age" were often referred to by the prophets.

g. Lit. "your arm," a figure of speech found in the prophets, Is 51:9; 53:1, referring to the miracles of the Exodus.

Psalm 72

a. This psalm dedicated to Solomon whose wealth, glory, and just and peaceful reign it celebrates (1 K 3:9, 12, 28; 4:20; 10:1–29; 1 Ch 22:9), evokes the image of the future ideal king. Jewish and Christian tradition see it as a portrait of the messianic King foretold by Isaiah, 9:5; 11:1–5, and Zechariah, 9:9f.

b. Division of verse according to Greek. Text uncertain.

c. "He will endure" Greek; "they will fear you" Hebr.

d. The versions translate "fleece," cf. Jg 6:37f.

e. "virtue" MSS and versions; "the virtuous man" Text. Rec., cf. Jr 23:5; Zc 9:9.

f. The messianic age will last to the end of time.

g. The boundaries of an ideal Palestine, cf. Jg 20:1+.

h. The word, meaning the animals or demons of the desert, Is 13:21; 34:14; Jr 50:39; Ezk 34:28, here refers to subjugated heathen states, cf. Is 27:1; Dn 7:3, etc.; Rv 13:1, etc.

i. Probably a prayer for the Messiah added later.

j. Another translation "He (the Messiah) will pray (intercede) for him (the poor man) and bless him."

k. "abundant," lit. "May it abound." "its harvest," lit. "putting forth" (or "making it rise"), misplaced in Hebr. to after "luxuriant" (lit. "may they [the mountains] be luxuriant"), is often translated "from the city" (Zion). Some interpret "May the inhabitants of Zion flourish."

l. "blessed" and "every race in the world": Greek; absent from Hebr. "enduring" one MS and versions; "branching forth is his name" Hebr., alluding to the messianic title "Branch," Is 4:2; Jr 23:5; 33:15; Zc 3:8; 6:12.

m. The colophon and preceding doxology close the second book of the Psalter.

Psalm 73

a. The poet-sage is troubled by the prosperity of the godless and the sufferings of the upright, cf. Jr 12:1f; Ml 3:15; Qo 7:15, etc.; Jb 21 etc., but goes on to contrast the passing pleasures of the sinner with the enduring peace of God's friendship.

b. It is possible that "Israel" is the result of dittography and that we ought to read "the virtuous man."

c. "the Lord" conj.; "and I" Hebr. (after "hearts").

d. "For them" corr.; "At their death" Hebr.

e. "spite" versions; "eye" Hebr. Fatness symbolizes the hardened heart.

f. Lit. "they set their mouth against heaven, their tongue goes about on earth."

g. Lit. "waters come to them in abundance." Verse translated according to versions. Meaning obscure. Possibly read "They are crammed with riches, and days (Greek) of plenty come to them."

h. Lit. "the sanctuaries of God." The psalmist is not referring to the Temple where God may have enlightened him, or to divine mysteries, Ws 2:22, revealed to him, but to the teaching contained

257

in the scriptures, dwelling place of wisdom, Pr 9:1f; Si 14:21f, and staple of Jewish piety, Si 39:1.

i. On God's "awakening," cf. 35:23; 44:23; 59:5; 78:65; Is 51:9. On the "phantom," or "shape," cf. 49:14; 90:5; Jb 20:8; Is 29:7–8.

j. Lit. "Behemoth," crassness personified, cf. Jb 40:15+.

k. Probably not a reference to heavenly glory (Enoch, Gn 5:24; Elijah, 2 K 2:3). The versions translate "with glory," giving the word its usual sense when used of men; this interpretation suggests that God preserves the just man from an early and shameful death and will vindicate him, even though the upright man dies while the wicked survive. Moreover, as in 16:9f, the psalmist yearns for unbreakable union with God; this is a milestone on the road to a formulated belief in resurrection and eternal life, cf. 16:10+.

l. Lit. "are fainting," i.e. with desire, cf. 84:2; Jb 19:27, not with weakness, cf. 143:7.

m. Lit. "those who are adulterous toward you." In prophetic literature the expression means infidelity to God.

n. Greek adds "in the gates of the daughter of Zion," cf. 9:14.

Psalm 74

a. According to the Targum, the "madman" (v. 22) is Antiochus Eipiphanes, the "mad king" who burned the Temple gates, 1 M 4:38; 2 M 1:8, and profaned the sanctuary, 1 M 1:21f, 39; 2 M 6:5. But the psalm can also apply to the sack of the Temple by the army of Nebuchadnezzar, 2 K 25:9; Is 64:10, from which epoch the voice of prophecy ceased, v. 9, cf. Ps 77:8; Lm 2:9; Ezk 7:26 and 1 M 4:46; 9:27; 14:41.

b. "entrance" versions.

c. Lit. "signs which they had not known" Greek; "signs; it is known" Hebr.

d. Lit. "(They have said in their heart,) 'let us destroy them'" cf. Syr.; "their offspring" Hebr.

e. Jeremiah had spoken of seventy years of exile, Jr 25:11; 29:10, a figure symbolizing long duration.

f. Lit. "why is your right hand kept in the grip of your bosom" corr.; "why is your right hand consumed from your bosom" Hebr.

g. Allusion to the crossing of the Reed Sea, Ex 14:30, and the defeat of the Egyptians, Ezk 29:3; 32:4.

h. "wild animals," lit. "to people, to animals."

i. Allusion to the miracles of the Exodus, Ex 17:1–7; Nb 20:2–13, and to the crossing of the Jordan, Jos 3, as manifestations of the power of the creator. This recapitulation of divine favors in the past, vv. 12–17, preludes the closing entreaty, vv. 18–23.

j. Hosea compared Israel to a dove, Ho 7:11; 11:11, cf. Sg 5:2. Greek and Syr. "the soul that gives you thanks."

Psalm 75

a. An antiphon, v. 1, introduces a divine oracle addressed to the wicked, and foretelling judgment on them, vv. 2–5. Vv. 6–8 describe the universal judgment at which the virtuous man rejoices, vv. 9–10.

b. "as we invoke your name, as we recount" versions; "near is your name, they recount" Hebr.

c. The horn is the symbol of arrogant or aggressive strength, 89:17; 92:10; Dt 33:17; 1 K 22:11; Zc 2:4.

d. "nor from the mountains" corr.; "(from the desert) of the mountains" Hebr. V. 6 names the four points of the compass, the "desert" being to the S., the "mountains" (of Lebanon) to the N. As in Zc 2:1, the emphasis is placed on the universality of the judgment on the day of Yahweh.

e. The image of the cup of wrath with its heady and stupefying wine, cf. 11:6+, is taken from the prophets, cf. Is 51:17+.

f. Lit. "he pours from it, only the dregs they drink"; Greek and Syr. suppose "he pours from one (cup) to the other."

Psalm 76

a. Eschatological hymn. Like 46 and 48:5, it apparently refers to the defeat of Sennacherib in 701 at the gates of Jerusalem, 2 K 19:35, which defeat is now symbolic of the rescue which the "humble" may hope for, v. 9. The Greek title includes "Concerning the Assyrian."

b. Abridged name of Jerusalem, cf. Gn 14:18; Jdt 4:4, the city of peace (*shalom*).

c. Lit. "flashings of the bow."

d. Others translate "the weapons of war."

e. Lit. "of mountains of spoil they were plundered." Hebr. interprets "majestic from the mountains of spoil"; Greek "from the everlasting mountains" (the same word means both "everlasting" and "spoil").

f. Lit. "under the strength (of your fury)" corr.; "since" Hebr.

g. Because God has frustrated the fury of the enemy.

h. The image, taken from Jeremiah, cf. 109:19, symbolizes close union. Like Terror (= the Terrible) in v. 11, the wrath of God is here apparently personified, cf. 58:9. The helpless "wrath" of man can only witness to the power and justice of God.

i. Like his "girdle," v. 10.

Psalm 77

a. In the hard times after the return from exile the psalmist recalls Yahweh's past favors to Israel, the miracles attending the Exodus from Egypt, as an earnest of Yahweh's future interventions on behalf of his people.

b. Lit. "I murmured" Greek, Syr.; "I will remember my lyre" Hebr. Vv. 5–6 here divided as in versions.

c. Lit. "what weakens me" Aquila and Jerome; "I am pierced" Hebr.

d. Lit. "I remember" versions; "I shall make known" Hebr. *ketib*.

e. Cosmic imagery, cf. Jb 7:12+, to describe the crossing of the Red Sea. V. 18 refers to the theophany of Sinai, Ex 19:16+.

Psalm 78

a. A didactic meditation, in the manner of Dt, on the history of Israel, the sins of the nation and their punishment. The psalm stresses the responsibility of Ephraim, the ancestor of the Samaritans, the choice of Judah and the call of David.

b. Parable (*mashal*): rhythmical maxim expressed in poetic parallelism.

c. The psalmist blames the sins of the nation on Ephraim, thus anticipating the future history of the Northern Kingdom (or possibly alluding to the Samaritan schism, cf. Zc 11:14). Cf. v. 67.

d. The miracles of the Exodus, vv. 12–31.

e. Lit. "the Mighty," i.e. the angels, cf. 103:20.

f. A general review, vv. 32–39, of the inconstancy of Israel and the patience of God.

g. Lit. "with haste" Greek.

h. The "plagues of Egypt," Ex 7:8+, summarized in vv. 43–51.

i. "plague" corr.; "hail" Hebr.

j. The Exodus from Egypt and invasion of Canaan, vv. 52–55.

k. The sins of Israel in the time of Samuel and Saul, vv. 56–64.

l. The ark of the covenant, 2 Ch 6:41; Ps 132:8.

m. Reference to the hemorrhoids inflicted on the Philistines when they had detained the ark.

n. Rejection of Ephraim, v. 67, choice of Zion, dwelling place of Yahweh and model of the heavenly sanctuary, vv. 68–69, and call of David, Yahweh's anointed, shepherd of his people and type of the awaited Messiah, vv. 70–72.

o. Lit. "Like the heights of heaven" corr.; "the high (beings)" Hebr.

Psalm 79

a. This psalm possibly refers to the capture of Jerusalem by the Chaldaeans in 587, and to the plundering of the city by Edom, Moab, and other neighboring powers, 2 K 24:2.

b. God is the "avenger of blood" for Israel, Nb 35:19+.

Psalm 80

a. This psalm could apply equally well either to N. Israel (cf. vv. 1–2) laid waste by the Assyrians (mentioned in the Greek title), cf. Jr 31:15f, or to Judah after the sack of Jerusalem in 586, cf. Jr 12:7–13. The psalmist looks forward to the reuniting of the king-dom, cf. Is 49:5; Ezk 37:16; Zc 9:13; 10:6, within its ideal frontiers, v. 11, cf. Jg 20:1+.

b. Ephraim and Manasseh, sons of Joseph, with whom Benjamin is sometimes reckoned, are the two principal tribes of the North.

c. "Yahweh Sabaoth" Syr.; "God" Hebr.

d. Hebr. adds "God." So also in v. 19.

e. Allegory frequent in the prophets, cf. Is 5:1+.

f. Or "the branches were cedars of God" (i.e. the highest of cedars, cf. 36:6; 68:15).

g. The Euphrates.

h. Hebr. adds "and on the son you authorized" (lit. "strength-ened") anticipation of 17b.

i. Line corr.

j. Probable allusion to Zerubbabel, Hg 1:1; Ezr 3:2, rather than to Benjamin ("son of the right hand"), Amaziah ("Yahweh is trusty") cf. 2 Chr 25:5, or Israel (cf. Ex 4:22).

Psalm 81

a. A prelude, vv. 1–5, introduces a divine oracle, cf. 50:95, in the style of Dt. The feast of Tabernacles, Ex 23:14+, commemorated the period in the desert and the Law given at Sinai. It was the greatest feast of the year.

b. The first day of the lunar month was a feast day, 2 K 4:23; Am 8:5; Ho 2:13; Is 1:13. The first day of the seventh month was long reckoned as the first day of the new year, Lv 23:24; Nb 29:1; at the full moon next following, the feast of Tabernacles was celebrated, Lv 23:34; Nb 29:12.

c. "against"; Greek interprets "from," making the subject not God but Joseph.

d. Greek and Syr. translate "He heard."

e. Allusion to the forced labor imposed on Israel in Egypt.

f. At the theophany of Sinai.

Psalm 82

a. A warning to wicked rulers and judges in an eschatological setting, vv. 1, 5, 8.

b. Indictment frequent in the prophets: Is 1:17f; Jr 5:28; 21:12; 22:3; Ezk 22:27, 29; Mi 3:1-11; Zc 7:9-10; cf. Jb 29:12; Pr 18:5; 24:11-12.

c. The rulers and judges are reckoned with the "sons of the Most High," the members of the heavenly court, cf. Jb 1:6+. Christ applies this passage, in a different context, to the Jews instructed by the word of God.

Psalm 83

a. Without naming any particular hostile coalition, the psalm enumerates ten traditional enemies of Israel whose hostility was maintained to a late date, cf. 2 Ch 20:1f; Ne 2:19, etc.; 1 M 5:3f.

b. Lit. "with one heart, and" corr.

c. Sons of Hagar, nomads of Transjordania.

d. Gebal: here Gabalene, district of Idumaea to the N. of Petra, and not Byblos as in Ezk 27:9.

e. Either Assyria (here perhaps standing for Seleucid Syria, cf. Jdt 16:3) or the Asshurite tribe, Gn 25:3, 2 S 2:9+; cf. Nb 24:22.

f. Or possibly "thistledown," the seed of which turns round and round as it flies.

Psalm 84

a. Song of Zion praising Yahweh as host in his Temple, dispensing happiness and forgiveness to pilgrims, vv. 5-7, and to all who serve in his sanctuary, vv. 4, 10.

b. "Ascents" Greek; "pathways" Hebr. The psalms entitled "Gradual" or "of Ascents," 120f, were sung by pilgrims on the march.

c. In seven MSS and in the versions "Valley of Tears," cf. Jg 2:5. The "Weeper" must here be the balsam tree (2 S 5:23-24). The "Valley of the Balsam tree," to the N. of the Ge-hinnom valley, was the last stage of the pilgrimage, the junction of roads coming from N., W., and S. Cf. 2 S 5:17-25.

d. Text uncertain. Greek "the lawgiver will bestow blessings." A possible correction "the leader will call out the blessings." We follow the Hebr. text. The allusion to the first rains of autumn make it

feasible to connect the psalm with the feast of Tabernacles, Ex
23:14+.

e. "from height to height"; others translate "from strength to
strength," or (Targ.) "from battlement to battlement." "soon . . .
Zion": lit. "God will appear to them in Zion"; for "God to them"
Hebr. has "the God of gods."

f. Hebr. inserts "God."

g. Here the "anointed" ("messiah") is probably the high priest,
chief authority in the post-exilic community.

h. The sons of Korah (cf. inscr.) were the gatekeepers (cf. 1 Ch
26:1).

i. Hebr. inserts "Yahweh" before "God." For "battlement" cf. Is
54:12.

Psalm 85

a. The psalm promises the returned exiles the peace of the
messianic age foretold by Isaiah and Zechariah.

b. The glory of Yahweh, Ex 24:16+, which had deserted the
Temple and the holy city, is to return to the restored Temple, Ezk
43:2; Hg 2:9.

c. Personified attributes of God; these will inaugurate the kingdom
of God on earth and in the hearts of men.

d. "Peace" conj.; "will put (his steps on the path)" Hebr.

Psalm 86

a. Lit. "there are no works like those you have made."

b. Hebr. here adds "you have made," words misplaced from the
preceding line.

Psalm 87

a. Holy Zion, the city of God, 2 S 5:9+, is to become the sacred
metropolis and mother of all peoples. All the pagan neighbors of
Israel: Egypt ("Rahab"), Ethiopia, Syro-Palestine, Mesopotamia, are
summoned to acknowledge the true God and to provide him with
converts. Such is the will of Yahweh as expressed in the oracle of
vv. 4–5. The psalm draws on Isaiah and Zechariah. Isaiah had already spoken of Zion as mother, fruitful spouse of Yahweh and, as
such, a foreshadowing of the Church.

b. Lit. "He says (Hebr. 'it is said') glorious things."

c. "Mother" Greek; absent from Hebr.

d. The pagans, wherever born, are adopted by Zion, which becomes their true country.

e. Reference to the roll of citizenship, Is 4:3; Ezk 13:9, not to the apocalyptic book of dooms, Ps 69:28. The pagans are listed as citizens of Zion.

f. "princes" MSS and versions; "singers" Text. Rec. "dancing there," lit. "as dancers." The nations are made freemen of the city and their princes are allowed to sing and dance in her sacred liturgy, 149:3; 150:4; cf. 2 S 6:5.

g. Following Greek. Hebr. "all my water sources are in you."

Psalm 88

a. With this anguished prayer, cf. the complaints of Job.

b. Text corr.; Hebr. "Yahweh, God of my salvation, on the day . . ."

c. Meaning uncertain. Greek "free." Others translate "my couch," "my place of imprisonment."

d. In Hebr. "Abaddon," Jb 26:6; 28:22; Pr 15:11; Rv 9:11.

Psalm 89

a. The prelude, vv. 1–2, followed by the rehearsal of the Davidic covenant, vv. 3–4, and a hymn to the creator, vv. 5–18, introduces a messianic oracle, vv. 19–37, and, in contrast, an account of the humiliations of the nation, vv. 38–45, concluded by a prayer, vv. 46–51. The pairing of "love" with "faithfulness" is a feature of this psalm.

b. "for I claim" lit. "I have said"; versions "you have said," "is built" versions; "you built" Hebr. "in the heavens" Greek (lit. "the heavens, in them").

c. Lit. "sons of the gods," i.e. the angels; so also the "holy ones" in v. 7.

d. "great" corr.; Hebr. joins "great" with "assembly."

e. A mythical monster personifying the watery chaos. cf. Jb 7:12+; it also sometimes means Egypt, Ps 87:4.

f. Lit. "lift up our horn."

g. Samuel and Nathan.

h. "crown" corr.; "help" Hebr.

i. A divine title here applied to God's anointed king.

j. Here the word indicates the whole Davidic dynasty.

k. Lit. "what duration" text uncertain.

l. "taunts" cf. Syr.

m. Doxology terminating the third book of the Psalter.

Psalm 90

a. A sage's meditation on the shortness of human life made shorter still by sin, cf. Gn 3.

b. "refuge" MSS and versions; "dwelling place" Hebr.

c. Hebr. has "you sweep them away, a dream they are, in the morning like . . ."

d. Lit. "like a sigh" Hebr.; Syr. "spider," a word added in Greek and Vulg.

e. Lit. "but most of them" corr.

f. "fear the violence" corr.

g. Awareness of human weakness leads to wisdom, which is fear of God, Pr 1:7+.

h. In vv. 14–17, the meditation and prayer, concerned initially with the fate of the individual, are extended to the whole of Israel.

i. Hebr. adds, after "Lord," "our God" and, in conclusion, "over us, and make the work of our hands succeed."

Psalm 91

a. This psalm elaborates the traditional teaching of the Sages, cf. Jb 5:19f, on God's protection of the virtuous man. The concluding divine oracle, vv. 14–16, assumes that the virtuous will be tested, but that God will deliver them.

b. Four divine names in this one strophe: Elyon ("the Most High"), Shaddai (Gn 17:1+; here translated "the God of heaven" by Greek and Vulg., elsewhere "the Almighty"), Yahweh (Ex 3:14+), Elohim (God).

c. "you" (lit. "he") versions; "I" Hebr.

d. "hoping to destroy" (lit. "who speaks of destroying") corr.; "from the plague" Hebr.; "from the word" versions (so also in v. 6).

e. "that wreaks havoc in broad daylight" (lit. "noon"); versions "from the noonday devil."

f. "you who can say" corr.; "you" Hebr. "fortress" Greek; "dwelling place" Hebr.

g. Greek and Syr. "asp."

Psalm 92

a. Lit. "exalted" corr. Hebr. adds "Yahweh."

b. Hebr. has "See how your enemies, Yahweh, see how your enemies perish."

c. "you pour" Syr.

d. Versions "my enemies." Hebr. adds "those who rise up against me."

Psalm 93

a. The sovereignty of God, displayed by the laws he imposes on the physical world, and the Law which he gives to man. According to the title in Greek and Talmud, this psalm was recited "on the eve of the sabbath, when the earth was inhabited" (cf. Gn 1:24–31).

b. "You have made firm" corr., "is set firm" Hebr.; "He laid the foundations of," versions.

c. The heavens are the palace of God, 8:2, etc. The "waters," vv. 3–4, probably represent those powers hostile to God and his people, cf. Jb 7:12+; Ps 18:4+; Is 8:7; 17:12; Dn 7:2; Rv 17:15.

d. "Yahweh" is not found in Hebr.

e. Lit. "more majestic than" corr.; "majestic" Hebr.

f. These "decrees" are the revealed Law, as immutable as the physical universe, and the basis of Yahweh's absolute sovereignty over Israel, as over the creation.

g. I.e. the Temple, consecrated for ever, 1 K 8:13; 9:3, and consecrating all who approach the holy God there, Ex 19:6+; Lv 10:3; 19:2; Ezk 42:14.

Psalm 94

a. This psalm expresses the traditional teaching of the sages, in the manner of Pr.

b. In the broadest sense: of revelation and moral teaching.

c. I.e. Sheol.

Psalm 95

a. Allusion, repeated in v. 8, to the rock that yielded water in the desert, Ex 17:1f, or to the rock on which the Temple was built, 2 S 24:18.

b. Lit. "of his hand."

c. Meribah means "dispute," Massah "temptation."

d. "that" versions; omitted by Hebr.

Psalm 96

a. A hymn, possibly combining two poems, in honor of the sovereignty of God and of his coming as judge of the world, is composed of material from psalms and from Is. The order is different in the version of 1 Ch 16:23–33.

b. Greek here translates "the demons." This theme appears frequently in the second part of Is (40:18f) etc. Cf. 1 Co 8:4+.

c. The poet adapts 29:1–2 and stresses the universalist aspect, cf. Zc 14:17; Ps 47:9.

d. "bear it" corr., cf. 1 Ch; "enter into his courts" (cf. Ps 95:6) Hebr.

e. "court" versions; "adornment" Hebr.

Psalm 97
a. Eschatological hymn with numerous reminiscences of other psalms.

b. Hebr. adds "before Yahweh."

c. I.e. the other towns of Judah.

d. Lit. "loves the man who hates" corr.; "those who love (Yahweh) hate" Hebr.

e. "dawns" versions; "is sown" Hebr.

Psalm 98
a. Eschatological hymn, inspired by the closing chapters of Is, and very similar to Ps 96.

b. Hebr. adds "and sing."

c. These fanfares, reserved in Israel for the accession of a new king, 2 S 15:10; 1 K 1:34, accompany the enthronement of Yahweh, Ps 47:5, for whom they had rung out on Sinai, Ex 19:16.

Psalm 99
a. Eschatological hymn, the two parts of which, vv. 1–4, 6–8, end with a refrain, vv. 5 and 9, celebrating the holiness of the King of Israel.

b. "mighty" corr.; "the might (of the king)" Hebr.

c. The great intercessors, cf. Ex 32:11+; Nb 17:11–13; Ps 106:23.

Psalm 100
a. Cf. Mt 19:17.

b. An ancient refrain, Jr 33:11, often repeated in Ps as antiphon or prelude, and quoted in 2 Ch 5:13; 7:3; 20:21; Ezr 3:11; Jdt 13:21 (Vulg.); 1 M 4:24. Cf. Mi 7:20.

Psalm 101
a. Portrait of the virtuous ruler; reminiscent of several passages in Pr.

b. Thus the versions; possibly alluding to the expected coming of the Messiah, "he who comes," Mt 11:3; Jn 4:25. Or "When you come to me."

c. Lit. "Each morning." Morning is the hour of divine favors, 17:15+, as also of human and divine justice, 2 S 15:2; Jr 21:12; Zp 3:5; Is 33:2; Jb 7:18; Ps 46:5; 73:14.

Psalm 102

a. This psalm of repentance combines two poems of differing rhythm: a personal complaint, inscr. to v. 11 and 23–27, cf. 69, and a prayer for the restoring of ruined Zion, vv. 12–22 and 28 (we transpose v. 28 to before v. 21).

b. Lit. "and I groan"; "I am" Hebr.

c. "those who used to praise me" MSS and versions; "those who deride me" Text. Rec.

d. I.e. as a sample of the fate they wish for their enemies, cf. Jr 29:22.

e. "God"; Hebr. "Yah."

f. "my strength has run out" corr.

g. Lit. "tell me what few days I have" versions; "he has shortened my days; I say: My God" Hebr.

h. Lit. "you (are) he."

Psalm 103

a. "your years" (or "your existence") corr.; "your adornment" Hebr.

b. The eagle was credited with long life, and renewal of strength after molting.

c. These are attributes of the name of Yahweh which were revealed to Moses, Ex 34:6+; the psalm develops these throughout, stressing mercy and kindness, cf. vv. 17–18 and Ex 20:6, thus preparing for 1 Jn 4:8.

Psalm 104

a. This hymn follows the sequence of the creation narrative in Gn 1.

b. Lit. "the thirsty wild donkeys hope for them (i.e. the springs)" corr.

c. "your heavens" corr.; "your works" Hebr.

d. "on the highest branches" cf. Greek.

e. Probably the hyrax, cf. Pr 30:26.

f. The spirit of God is the source of all being and life.

g. Hebr. places here the "Alleluia" which Greek has at the beginning of 105.

Psalm 105

a. The psalm successively recalls the story of the patriarchs, vv. 8–15, the story of Joseph, vv. 16–23, the mission of Moses,

vv. 24–27, the plagues of Egypt, vv. 28–36, the Exodus and journey through the wilderness, vv. 37–43, and finally the entry into Canaan, the land promised to Abraham, vv. 44–45.

b. "his chosen one" two MSS; "his chosen ones" Text. Rec.

c. The metaphor of the "staff of bread" occurs in Ezk 4:16; 5:16; 14:13 and Lv 26:26.

d. "to train" versions; "to bind" Hebr.

e. Lit. "they performed"; versions "he performed."

f. "they defied" versions; "they did not defy" Hebr.

Psalm 106

a. Vv. 1–5 and 48 provide a liturgical setting for a historical psalm, inspired by Dt and Nb, forming a national confession, in which the repentant nation rehearses its collective sins committed in the past and confesses them to God. Cf. 1 K 8:33–34; Is 63:7–64:11; Ne 9:5–37; Dn 9; Ba 1:15–3:8.

b. "the Most High" conj.; "at the sea" Hebr.

c. Word of uncertain meaning. Greek translates "a glut."

d. "embittered" corr.; "rebelled against (God's spirit)" Hebr.

e. Prophetic expression for apostasy and idolatry.

f. Closing doxology to the fourth book of the Psalter; followed by a liturgical rubric.

Psalm 107

a. Hymn of thanksgiving, inspired by the second part of Is, for the mercies of Providence: the Exodus, vv. 4–9, the return from exile, vv. 10–16, the help given to those who suffer, vv. 17–22, and to those on the high seas, vv. 23–32. The epilogue, vv. 33–43, elaborates the wisdom theme of the reversal of situations. There is a two-part refrain: vv. 6 and 8, 13 and 15, 19 and 21, 28 and 31.

b. "south" corr.; "sea" Hebr. This prelude calls on the returned exiles to praise God.

c. Probable reference to Canaan. The Exodus and the installation in the Promised Land had already, in Is 40f, served as prototype of the return from exile.

d. Lit. "their life from the pit" corr.

Psalm 108

a. With a few variants an editor has combined 57:7–11 and 60:5–12. See notes to these psalms.

Psalm 109

a. Slandered and falsely accused, the psalmist invokes divine venge-ance, cf. Jr 11:20; 18:19f and Ps 5:10+. In the oriental manner, the litany of imprecations, 6–20, piles up highly colored curses. Perhaps vv. 6–15 (within quotation marks here) express the accuser's enmity, cf. vv. 2–3, and what follows is the psalmist's retort, invoking the law of retaliation, vv. 16–20, cf. Ex 21:25+.

b. Lit. "and I a prayer."

c. Lit. "let the accuser stand at his right hand." The Accuser (Hebr. *satan*) was a name later given to the devil, cf. Jb 1:6+. He, like the advocate, v. 31, stands on the right of the accused, Zc 3:1; Jb 30:12.

d. Greek; Hebr. "seeking."

e. Hebr. adds "before Yahweh."

f. "recoil on," "shun" versions; Hebr. has past tenses. Curse and blessing are here personified.

g. Probable allusion to the trial by water described in Nb 5:11–31.

h. Lit. "my heart writhes in me"; "writhes" versions; "is wounded" Hebr.

i. Lit. "I am shaken out like a locust." Possibly, helpless as a locust blown by the wind; more probably "shaken off" from life.

Psalm 110

a. The prerogatives of the Messiah, worldwide sovereignty and perpetual priesthood, cf. 2 S 7:1+; Zc 6:12–13, are no more con-ferred by earthly investiture than were those of the mysterious Mel-chizedek, Gn 14:18+. V. 1 is accepted in the N.T. epistles and else-where as a prophecy of the ascension of Christ to the right hand of the Father.

b. The risen Christ is seated at the right hand of the Father, Rm 8:34; Heb 10:12; 1 P 3:22.

c. Cf. Jos 10:24; Dn 7:14.

d. Zion; the plural is "of majesty," cf. 87:1 (Hebr.).

e. Verse corr.; Hebr. "Your people is generosity on the day of your strength, in sacred splendors, from (or: from the time of) the womb of the dawn (meaning uncertain), to you the dew of youth." Greek "With you is the royal dignity . . . , from the womb before the dawn I begot you" (cf. Hebr. MSS, and 2:7). Many Hebr. MSS, Symmachus and Jerome have "on the holy mountains." We correct "your strength" (Hebr.) to "you were born" (lit. "your birth").

f. As the text stands, this is addressed to the Messiah: the Lord

(Yahweh) is to be at his right hand. Possibly the original text attributed the following act of judgment to the Messiah himself, and we should read "At his (Yahweh's) right hand the Lord (the Messiah, as in v. 1)." This text may have been corrected in order to reserve the functions of eschatological judge as described in the following lines. However this may be, Jesus, the Messiah and Son of God, claimed this right to judge as his own, Mt 24:30; 26:64; Jn 5:22; cf. Ac 7:56; 10:42; 17:31.

g. As for the following verbs, so here the subject seems to be not Yahweh but the Messiah.

h. "skulls" Greek; in the singular (collective?) in Hebr. "he gives . . . corpses": lit. "he heaps up corpses, he smashes skulls over the wide world" (versions "skulls of man").

i. The Messiah drinks of the torrent of ordeal, 18:4+; 32:6; 66:12, or of the torrent of divine favors, 36:8; 46:4. Or possibly he is compared to the warrior pursuing his enemies, pausing only a moment to quench his thirst, Jg 7:5; 15:18; 1 S 30:9.

j. The text is applied to the suffering and glorified Christ, cf. Ph 2:7–11.

Psalm 111

a. "Alphabetical" psalm, like the following which is akin to it in doctrine, style, and poetic structure.

b. By instituting the yearly feasts, cf. Ex 23:14+.

c. Allusion to the miracles of manna and quails, Ex 16:1+.

Psalm 112

a. Expressions used of God in the preceding psalm are here applied to the virtuous man.

b. The word indicates both the virtue and the happiness that rewards it.

c. Lit. "he rises." What has been said of God, 18:28; 27:1, is here applied to the virtuous man. Others translate "For the virtuous man in darkness a light arises; the upright man is kind and compassionate."

d. Lit. "his horn is exalted in honor."

Psalm 113

a. Opening hymn of the Hallel (Ps 113–118) which the Jews recited at the great feasts, including the Passover supper, cf. Mt 26:30f.

b. Like Sarah, Gn 16:1; 17:15–21; 18:9–15; 21:1–7, and Hannah, 1 S 1–2.

Psalm 114

a. This hymn, which the versions wrongly unite with the following, treats in parallel, cf. 66:6+, of the crossing of the Red Sea and the crossing of the Jordan, Ex 14 and Jos 3.

b. Greek. Hebr. puts the "Alleluia" at the end of the preceding psalm.

Psalm 115

a. "and on earth" Greek; omitted by Hebr.

b. These three groups appear again in 118:2–4, "those who fear Yahweh" are the proselytes, cf. 15:4+.

c. Versions "he has blessed us."

Psalm 116

a. "Alleluia" Greek; Hebr. puts it at the end of the preceding psalm.

b. Lit. "on the day" Syr.; "in my days" Hebr.

c. "nooses" Jerome; "sorrow" Hebr. Hebr. adds "I undergo" at the end.

d. "He has" versions; "you (sing.) have" Hebr.

e. This verse is to be read after v. 17; it has been attracted to v. 8 under the influence of the parallel 56:13. Vulgate Ps 115 begins at the following verse.

f. Thanksgiving ritual preserved in Jewish and Christian liturgy. Cf. 1 Co 10:16.

g. Lit. "is precious in the sight of Yahweh"; death severed all contact between them and him, cf. Ps 6:5+. The versions interpret this text in the light of the dogma of the resurrection "Precious in the sight of God is the death of his saints" which in the liturgy concludes the reading of the Martyrology, and recalls the "birth in heaven" of the martyrs.

Psalm 117

a. "Alleluia" Greek; Hebr. puts it with preceding psalm.

Psalm 118

a. This psalm ends the Hallel, cf. 113:1+. An invitatory, vv. 1–4, precedes the hymn of thanksgiving put into the mouth of the personified community, and is followed by a number of versicles and responses, vv. 19f, 25f, chanted by various groups as the procession entered the Temple. The psalm may have been used for the feast described in Ne 8:13–18, cf. Ezr 3:4; Zc 14:16 and Ex 23:14+. Cf. also Ezr 3:11.

b. "Alleluia" Greek; Hebr. puts it with preceding psalm.

c. "the House" Greek; absent from Hebr.

d. Some translate "I cause them to be circumcised" (John Hyrcanus forced circumcision on the Idumaeans and Greeks).

e. "blazed" Greek; "were extinguished" Hebr.

f. "I was pressed" versions; "You pressed me" Hebr.

g. Versions "The right hand of the Lord has raised me up."

h. The Temple is rebuilt, cf. Hg 1:9; Zc 1:16. The "keystone" (or "crowning stone"), cf. Jr 51:26, that may become "a stone of stumbling," is a messianic theme, Is 8:14; 28:16; Zc 3:9; 4:7, applied to Christ, Mt 21:42f; Ac 4:11; Rm 9:33; 1 P 2:4f, cf. Ep 2:20; 1 Co 3:11.

i. In the Christian liturgy this verse is sung on Easter Day.

j. Ritual cry (*Hosanna:* "Oh, grant salvation!") to which the priests answer with a blessing. The acclamation was taken up by the crowds on Palm Sunday and is incorporated in the Sanctus of the Roman Mass.

k. Lit. "Inaugurate the ceremony with branches up to the horns of the altar!" Ritual of the *lulab,* branch of myrtle or palm, waved as the procession circled the altar.

Psalm 119

a. "Alphabetical" psalm. The eight verses of each strophe begin with one of the twenty-two letters of the Hebr. alphabet and each verse (excepting only v. 122) contains one of the terms for the Law: decree, precept, statute, commandment, promise, word, judgment, way. The word "law" and its synonyms are here to be understood in the widest sense of revealed teaching, as handed on by the prophets. The psalm is one of the most remarkable monuments of Israelite devotion to the divine revelation.

b. "Life" in this psalm is to be understood in its fullest sense: happiness, security, liberation; a theme recurrent in Ezk 3:21; 18; 33. Cf. Ps 133:3 and Dt 4:1, etc.

c. The greatest of God's enemies, vv. 51, 69, 78, 85, 122; 19:13; 86:14; Is 13:11; Ml 3:19.

d. Or "remove from me" versions; "uncover" Hebr.

e. "your statutes" Greek; absent in Hebr.

f. Lit. "I have desired" Syr.; "I have put (your rulings)" Hebr. "I have not forgotten" Greek.

g. Faithfulness to the commandments is the joy and immediate reward of the upright.

h. A wish often repeated in this psalm and reiterated by the sages.

i. "by your word" MSS, Targ.; "in your path" Text. Rec.

j. Gesture of veneration, cf. 44:20.

k. Which, after hanging in the house, shrivels and blackens.

l. Lit. "My soul in my hands continually"; the psalmist is prepared to sacrifice his life if necessary.

m. Lit. "I have regard for your statutes"; versions "I shall take delight in your statutes."

n. "Yahweh" one MS and Jerome; "for Yahweh" Text. Rec.

o. With Greek and Jerome.

p. Lit. "according to your promise" MSS and Greek; "in your promise" Text. Rec.

q. "Zeal for your house" Greek; "My zeal" Hebr.

r. With versions; "those who pursue (malice)" Hebr.

s. Lit. "be my redeemer."

t. Lit. "head."

u. The "lost sheep" theme of the prophets, Ezk 34:1+, is here applied to the individual.

Psalm 120

a. The "Songs of Ascents" (Ps 120–134) were probably sung by pilgrims on their way to Jerusalem, cf. 84:6+; Is 30:29. With the exception of 132 their verses are "elegiac" (unequal lines: 3+2 accents) and the "stair" device is often used (a verse takes up a word or expression from its predecessor, cf. 120:2–3, 5, 6, and 7).

b. Lit. "What will he give you and add to you?", a formula corresponding to the imprecatory oath, Rt 1:17+.

c. The country of the Moschoi, a Caucasian people, Gn 10:2; Ezk 27:13, where Gog is later to be king, Ezk 38:2. The Arabs of Kedar lived in the Syrian desert. The psalmist makes "Meshech" and "Kedar" synonymous with "barbarian."

d. Lit. "I, peace; but when I speak."

Psalm 121

a. This psalm is equally appropriate for pilgrims on the hard road to Jerusalem, as for those on their pilgrimage to the heavenly Jerusalem.

Psalm 122

a. The pilgrims halt at the gates and salute the holy city with "*Shalom!*" ("*Peace!*"), alluding to the popular etymology of "Jerusalem," "city of peace," cf. 76:2. This "peace" plays a prominent part in the messianic hope, cf. Is 11:6+; Ho 2:20+. Affection for holy Zion, 2 S 5:9+, is a characteristic of Jewish piety, cf. 48; 84; 87; 133; 137.

b. Jerusalem solidly restored, Ne 2:17f, is a symbol of the unity of the chosen people (versions "that is one in fellowship") and a type of the unity of the Church.

c. Lit. "Tents" corr. (one MS; cf. Jb 12:6).

Psalm 123

a. Probably composed shortly after the return from exile or in the time of Nehemiah; the restored community was exposed to the contempt and hostility of surrounding pagans, cf. Ne 2:19; 3:36.

b. Lit. "for the proud," meaning uncertain.

Psalm 124

a. Thanksgiving for dangers overcome, described in conventional metaphors.

Psalm 125

a. With Greek and Vulg.; Hebr. "He will not permit a scepter of the wicked to fall."

Psalm 126

a. For the returned exiles faced with the difficulties of reconstruction (cf. Ne 5, etc.), the return from Babylon portends the coming of the messianic age.

b. Which, nearly always dry, cf. Jb 6:15, fill swiftly in winter and fertilize the soil.

Psalm 127

a. Without God, man's work is useless; daily bread and children are gifts from God.

b. Lit. "he gives to his loved one in sleep," or "he gives sleep"; versions "while he gives sleep to those he loves." The Hebr. title of the psalm identifies the "loved one" with Solomon, cf. 2 S 12:25, and possibly the "sleep" with Solomon's dream at Gibeon, 1 K 3:5.

c. Lit. "when he speaks with his enemies in the gate," i.e. the gate of the city, where business is transacted.

Psalm 128
a. This psalm celebrates the domestic happiness granted by God to the virtuous, in accordance with the teaching of the sages on earthly retribution.

Psalm 129
a. The early days of Israel's history: the years in Egypt and the entry into Canaan.
b. Lit. "(let them be like grass) that the east wind blasts" conj.; "before it is gathered it dries up" Hebr.

Psalm 130
a. Penitential Psalm, cf. 6: inscr., but still more a psalm of hope; it takes a prominent place in the Christian liturgy for the dead, not as a lament but as an expression of trust in God the Redeemer.
b. Lit. "that you may be feared"; Greek "because of your law."
c. The text of vv. 5–7 is disordered. Greek "5 I await you, Lord, my soul awaits your word; 6 my soul relies on the Lord, from dawn watch to night (Jerome and Syr.: to morning watch). 7 From dawn watch let Israel rely on the Lord."

Psalm 131
a. The soul at peace abandons itself to God, laying aside anxiety and ambition. The same childlike trust is demanded, v. 3, of the people of God, cf. Is 30:15.

Psalm 132
a. Messianic psalm, cf. especially vv. 17–18. The divine promises, 2 S 7:1+, here take the form of the divine answer to an oath pronounced by David. A processional hymn, vv. 6f, recalls the finding and translation of the ark, 1 S 6:13f; 2 S 6.
b. The ark.
c. Place name akin to Kiriath-jearim ("town of the woodlands") which, like Bethlehem, was in the district of Ephrathah.
d. Yahweh.
e. "her virtuous" conj.; "her provisions" Hebr.
f. Cf. 1 K 11:36; 15:4; 2 K 8:19; 2 Ch 21:7. On the extinguished lamp, cf. Jr 25:10; Jb 18:5. The Messiah will be the light of the nations, Is 42:6; 49:6; Lk 2:32.

g. Greek and Syr. "my."

Psalm 133
a. The brotherly relationships binding priests and Levites in the Temple and holy city.
b. Text corr.

Psalm 134
a. Call to prayer, or liturgical dialogue between pilgrims and Temple ministers, perhaps used at a nocturnal ceremony inaugurating the feast of Tabernacles, cf. Ex 23:14+.
b. With Greek; line omitted by Hebr.
c. With this liturgical blessing, cf. Nb 6:23f, the series of "Songs of Ascents" comes to an end, 120:1+.

Psalm 135
a. Song of praise, composed entirely of reminiscences of, or borrowings from, the psalms or from other texts.

Psalm 136
a. This litany, cf. Dn 3:52–90, is called by the Jews "the Great Hallel"; at the Passover meal it was recited after the "Lesser Hallel," Ps 113–118.
b. "Alleluia" Greek; Hebr. joins it with preceding psalm.

Psalm 137
a. This psalm recalls the fall of Jerusalem in 587 and the Babylonian exile.
b. Following Targum.
c. "wither" corr.; "forget" Hebr.
d. The ninth day of the fourth month (June–July 587), when the Chaldaeans breached the walls of Jerusalem, Jr 39:2; 52:7; or else the tenth day of the fifth month when the Temple was burnt down, Jr 52:13, cf. Zc 7:5; 8:19. The Edomites, Nb 20:23+, then joined forces with the besieging army; a number of prophetic oracles invokes the vengeance of Yahweh on them, Jr 49:17; Is 34:5f; Ml 1:3f; Jl 4:19.
e. Lit. "destroyer" versions; "destroyed" Hebr.

Psalm 138
a. Greek. Line omitted by Hebr.

b. With Greek and Vulg. Some versions interpret "gods" (idols), "kings," "judges."

c. Lit. "you have made your promise great above all your name." Text uncertain.

d. Lit. "gave more strength in my soul" versions.

e. Hebr. divides "and your right hand saves me. Yahweh will do everything for me."

Psalm 139

a. Cf. this meditation on God's omniscience with the reflections of Job on the fear of man under the eye of God, Jb 7:17–20+.

b. "cover" Symmachus and Jerome; "crush" Hebr.

c. The text adds an Aramaic gloss "As the darkness, so the light."

d. Hebr. lit. "I am wonderful, your works are wonderful."

e. Lit. "you know my soul" corr.; "my soul knows it" Hebr.

f. Lit. "in the depths of the earth."

g. Lit. "my actions" cf. Syr.; "my embryo" Hebr.

h. On this theme, cf. Rv 20:12+.

i. "my days" Targum; "the days" Hebr.

j. Lit. "appeared" conj.

k. Lit. "when I reach the end" 3 MSS; "when I awake" Hebr.

l. Either "I should still be conscious of God's presence"; or "I should still be faced with the mystery of God."

Psalm 140

a. Lit. "for my feet" Greek; omitted by Hebr.

b. Text corrected, cf. Greek; Hebr. divides differently.

c. Lit. "may it rain coals of fire": "may it rain" corr. "of fire" Greek.

d. Lit. "the man of tongue."

Psalm 141

a. A prescribed daily offering. Jewish piety thus associates prayer with sacrifice, cf. 51:16; cf. Rv 5:8; 8:4.

b. With Greek, Syr. and Hebr. MSS; "excellent oil let not my head decline it" Hebr.

c. Meaning of this and the following obscure.

d. The word may indicate God the Rock (95:1, etc.) who crushes the wicked.

e. "a millstone smashed" cf. Greek and Syr.; "shattering and splitting (the ground)" Hebr.

f. "their" Syr.; "his" Hebr.

Psalm 142

a. This psalm has been applied to Christ in his sufferings.

b. Versions "I look to the right hand." A man's advocate stands on his right.

c. This earth, cf. 27:13.

d. Lit. "(the virtuous will) gather round"; Greek and Syr. "hope."

Psalm 143

a. Cf. 51:5; 130:3. St. Paul uses this passage somewhat freely, Rm 3:20; Ga 2:16.

b. "I have fled" Greek.

Psalm 144

a. The first half, vv. 1–11, a summary of liturgical prayers for the king, is inspired by 18 and other psalms. The second, vv. 12–15, is original and describes the prosperity of the messianic age.

b. "David my servant" has become a messianic title, Jr 33:21; Ezk 34:23–24; 37:24.

c. Rare word suggesting caryatids.

Psalm 145

a. Text corr. Hebr. "the glory of your renown."

b. Versions "Let them tell, let them tell the story of your marvelous deeds."

c. The Nun verse is omitted in Hebr. but preserved in the versions.

d. Cf. Greek.

Psalm 146

a. This is the first psalm of a third Hallel, Ps 146–150, recited by Jews in the morning; cf. 113–118 and 136.

Psalm 147

a. Though divided into two (after v. 11) in several Hebr. versions, including Vulg., the psalm forms one poem. The poet celebrates God as the liberator of Israel, the creator, and friend of the lowly.

b. "Alleluia" Greek; Hebr. joins it with preceding psalm.

c. Hebr. adds "(praise) is befitting," omitted by Greek.

d. This line (Greek; cf. 104:14) is absent from Hebr.

e. The Fathers apply this second part of the psalm to the new Jerusalem, militant or triumphant.

f. The word of God is represented here as a messenger, almost as a person. Cf. 107:20; Is 55:11; Jn 1:14+.

Psalm 148

a. Greek and Vulg. here add 33:9a.

b. Lit. "raising a horn for."

Psalm 149

a. This national hymn looks to the eschatological future, cf. Is 61:2f, when Israel will be the instrument of divine justice, cf. Zc 9:13–16.

b. Lit. "on their couches," i.e. from the place where they lie prostrate in worship, cf. 95:6; Jdt 6:18; or it may mean: praise that does not cease, even at night. Cf. Ho 7:14; Ps 4:4; 63:6.

c. Allusion to the "Oracles against the Nations" in the prophetic books.

Psalm 150

a. A more elaborate doxology than those concluding the first four books of the Psalter, 41:13; 72:18–20; 89:51; 106:48; this one invites every musical instrument and every living being to praise Yahweh.

T39